Dundee
City Council
& Communities
CHANGIN
FOR THE FUTU
AND BUS

CANCELLED

# A Mini Adventure

# A MINI ADVENTURE

## 50 Years of the Iconic Small Car

Martin Wainwright

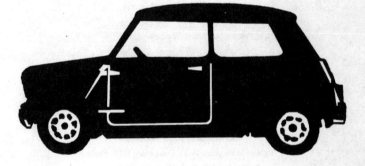

To Tom and Abi, starting out

First published in Great Britain
2009 by Aurum Press Ltd
7 Greenland Street
London NW1 0ND
www.aurumpress.co.uk

ISBN 978 1 84513 471 6

# Contents

| | | |
|---|---|---:|
| | Acknowledgements | vi |
| 1 | The IKEA Job | 1 |
| 2 | Born from a Bubble | 22 |
| 3 | Bill Cull to the Rescue | 43 |
| 4 | Trouble in Minitown | 60 |
| 5 | A Stuttering Star | 79 |
| 6 | Saved by the Swells | 100 |
| 7 | Super Cooper | 122 |
| 8 | Miniculture | 140 |
| 9 | The Long, the Short and the Tall | 168 |
| 10 | Near and Far | 196 |
| 11 | New MINI | 217 |
| | Select Bibliography | 239 |
| | Index | 240 |

# Acknowledgements

IF THIS BOOK HAS SOMEHOW SURVIVED for a thousand years, and you, the reader in AD 3000, are wondering what it was like to sit in, or even drive, a Mini, then I can help you. Not by describing the experience, although I try to do that in the pages which follow, but by directing you to the town of Guildford in Surrey, England, which I hope has survived into your time. Locate the castle, some of whose stones will certainly still be there, and start digging where old maps refer to Millbrook and Quarry Street. Not very far down, albeit beneath a layer of concrete, you should find Guildford Borough Council's Millennium Vault.

Guildford Borough Council may not exist in AD 3000, but it gave instructions that the vault should be opened in that year, after the steel doors were welded shut in March 2000 by Dame Vera Lynn, a famous woman of our time. So you should not get into trouble if you light-sabre or teleport your way into the gloom, all 100 cubic metres of it, which was specially treated and made airtight before the doors slammed shut. So were all the individual items, which, decay permitting, you should discover inside. They include photographs of the twenty women considered most beautiful in our time, a selection of popular twenty-first century jokes which will baffle you and … a Mini.

Metallic blue and scarcely used, it has the best chance of all 5,387,862 specimens of the car produced of lasting for 1000 years. This book is their story, from Sir Alec Issigonis' secret workshop in Birmingham to a version with snow-tracks which ferried scientists around in Antarctica. Brrr! A Mini can be chilly enough on an ordinary day in Britain. Very warmly, by contrast, I would like to thank everyone who has helped me. All have been unfailingly generous with their time and knowledge, from my very own Mr Bean and his family who let me chauffeur them in their Mini, to women's rugby star Luan Read, who squashed her bottom on to a Cooper's parcel shelf to help win the Guinness World Record for cramming people in. You will meet most of them as we motor along, but may I also thank Dan Read of BBC *Top Gear* magazine, who put me on to *The Italian Job*'s stunt drivers, Claire Halford from GKN Driveline for information about Bill Cull and Steve Kimber of Leeds Classic Mini Owners' Club who couldn't have been more helpful.

Lots of books and even more websites have been devoted to the Mini and I would specially like to acknowledge all that I have learned from some in particular. There are two excellent biographies of Sir Alec Issigonis: *Issigonis: The Official Biography* by Gillian Bardsley and *Alec Issigonis: The Man who Made the Mini* by Jonathan Wood. They form part of an essential trio on the car with *The Mini Story* by the late Lawrence Pomeroy, friend and collaborator of Issigonis and a character in this book in his own right. Bardsley and Wood correct various errors in Pomeroy's dating of events and suchlike, but his book is full of character and eloquently speaks the language of the time. Austin Rover Online, http://austin-rover.co.uk, is the outstanding web equivalent of these books, and I have learned much from its contributors, especially about the production of the Mini overseas. The National Mini/MINI Owners Club, www.miniowners club.co.uk, has been as helpful as everyone else. As the opening quote to Chapter One suggests, there is a bonhomie, a sense of friendliness and fellow-feeling, which attaches to everyone involved with this car.

Of course that includes, finally, the team at Aurum, Dan Steward, Lydia Harley, Phoebe Clapham, Colin Hynson and especially Graham Coster, who suggested this book. This is in spite of the fact that his real loyalty is to the Nissan Micra, of which he drives a battered example. I hope that one day he will tell us the story of that car.

## Chapter One
## The IKEA Job

*'You can't say the word "Mini" without starting to smile.'*
*Respondent to advertising agency survey for BMW 2001*

 THIS IS MERLIN. He is twenty-eight years old. He is *so* small, and the rest of the world has become so big. Next to him in the multi-storey car park, and towering two feet above, is a Land Rover Discovery. The bearded head of its owner appears round the back of it. 'Aaaaah, a *real* Mini,' he says, eyes misting. 'I had three of those – just seeing it makes me come over all nostalgic.' He would still have one if he and his family hadn't invested in a caravan. Caravans have a habit of swinging any Mini attempting to tow them around like a cat.

The plan had been this: we get a classic Mini – in this case VYG 280X, an Austin Morris Mini A+, 1000cc, aka Merlin – paint it in the red, white and blue livery of *The Italian Job* and drive it out of its own age – the miniature Sixties – and into the ultimate test for our modern-day large-scale existence: IKEA. How would this tiny little thing measure up to the Flatpack Challenge? The mastermind was Graham Bean, a pharmaceutical manager from Yorkshire with TA experience in Iraq.

('What's that, boss?' his Iraqi colleagues had asked him when he'd hung up a Mini calendar in his office in Basra. 'That's a Mini,' he said. 'D'you have them here?' 'No, boss,' they answered, rolling their eyes.) The team was Michèle, Graham's wife, son David, and daughter Nicola. And Merlin had no hatchback, no folding rear seats, and an interior no more than eight foot by five. Time to start loading up the trolley.

'Shove it this way, is the answer,' says Graham, manfully holding up one end of a 4ft 6in flatpack box for a sofa-bed frame (the Lycksele range, named after a town in Lapland). 'No hang on,' interrupts Michèle. 'That's the wrong door; it's going to take up the whole of the driving seat.' Muffled on the bench seat at the back of the car, partly beside and partly underneath two Expedit shelf boxes (2ft 1in by 11ins), Nicola says something like, 'Mmmf ... I'm ... blllmphed ... mmfsquashed ...' Expedit is Swedish for 'fabulous', and it is truly fabulous that so much cardboard and so many people (three Beans plus the IKEA flatpacks) can fit into Sir Alec Issigonis' legendary, tiny space.

'How can it happen? Let's measure the car,' I suggest, and Michèle nips off to get one of the store's free metre-long tapes. The four of us, with David in charge, kneel down on the dusty floor of the multi-storey car park and lay out the measure two and a half times − 10ft 3ins from bumper to bumper. 'How about measuring the difference with that,' says Graham, sizing up the Land Rover Discovery. 'It's at least an IKEA trolley and a half longer.' 'Goodness! It's four feet six inches more at least! It's vast!'

Our measuring caper was all about checking out the

Lilliputian nature of the Mini in today's world: how do you shop? How do you make lorries see you? Why do you put up with a ride like bouncing on a mattress full of pebbles with your iPod playing white noise at full volume in both ears? But the fascinating thing about this famous car is that it was ever thus. When the very first came off the assembly line in 1959, our astonished parents and grandparents had exactly the same reaction as mine when I first met Merlin. They also measured the new arrival, the world's first real mini-car; they lined it up against the Morris Oxford or even the Austin A35 and said, 'Crikey, isn't it an absolute *titch*?' I was chatting to one of the very first of them, Christine Perry, a couple of months before I went shopping in West Yorkshire with Mr Bean ('No connection,' says Graham, who has developed a permanently good-natured response to quips since Rowan Atkinson created his notorious Mini-owner in 1990).

Christine was thirteen and stuck in the science labs at Colmer Farm secondary school in Longbridge, Birmingham, on a sweltering afternoon in the summer of 1959. It had been hot and dry for ages (something which Issigonis later blamed for his team's failure to spot floor leaks, which became as precious a part of the Mini's history as the Silver Lady bonnet statuette for Rolls Royces). Christine's eyes kept rolling up sleepily or straying towards the Lickey Hills where the little cars were even then being secretly tested, in disguise, at night. 'Then,' she told me, 'our science teacher Mr Druce gave up on explaining Boyle's Law and diverted the whole lesson. He suddenly started talking, with his face lit up, about this revolution in car design which was going on at the Works [the huge British Motor Corporation plant across the Bristol Road]. It was called transverse, which meant the engine went crossways, I've always remembered that. To be honest, it was a totally boring subject but he was on fire with it. He told us: "Right as I'm speaking now, the very first transverse engine is coming off the Line" [the Longbridge assembly line, well over a mile long, and visible from the school]. It meant everything to him.'

Cars in 1959 were like computers today: new developments tumbled out after one another. Motor-racing fascinated inventive young engineers; engines, suspension and driveline were accessible and malleable – handy enthusiasts could bend or ease metal in a way impossible with silicon chips. Mr Druce gathered pace, increased in volume and then pulled out some fuzzy sneak pictures, which he had got from someone who had known someone else who had been handed them by a third someone who worked somewhere near the isolated design workshop. This was a brick hut miles from anywhere, near N Gate in the South Experimental area: management at Longbridge mysteriously called it just the 'Issigonis Cell'.

'Everyone knew someone in the Works,' said Christine. 'We all lived in spitting distance and just about everyone seemed to work there: your auntie, your uncle and your cousins. I did myself, to start with. After I left school, I dealt with all the car sales to people who worked for the firm – they got them ever so much cheaper. We walked up there to shifts and back in a mass. It was like a huge caterpillar.' But in spite of that, the Cell kept its secrets. The antheap nature of the plant with its 20,000 employees didn't mean individual disloyalty and what Mr Druce had got hold of was not a complete blueprint of the coming car. Nor, for all the money Fleet Street might have offered, was he in the business of passing it on, except to stimulate his class's interest in science. 'He had most of the specs and everything but not an actual picture of the car,' Christine remembered. 'That was kept under wraps – they were good at that up at the works. It was covered in some kind of sheeting and you couldn't make it out. Mr Druce had a diagram of what they thought it would look like, but we didn't actually get to see one until the launch.'

So the excitement wasn't dulled when the great day came. Once the Mini was out, Christine and her friends shared in what was genuinely a national sensation. Longbridge naturally had a ringside view of the first cars, as their rounded little shapes were loaded up and carted off on transporters, some to the ports, others to Evans & Evans' swanky car showroom in the centre of Birmingham. But there were plenty on the local streets after a day or two, and a kid could actually get given a ride in those. 'We were sooooo unused to anything like it. They were sooooo small,' marvelled Christine. 'I've always blamed them for the way garages seemed to get smaller and harder to drive into without scrapes. But goodness, they were roomy inside. People really did start making those jokes straight away about how many elephants you can get in a Mini. They were the talk of the town: "You should see this new car. You'll be amazed." I remember the stick-on eyes people put at the back too. Everyone had those eyes. It made the cars look like little people.'

Vrrrrrm! Nyeeehrrrrm! Now we're in the Beans' Mini and pulling away from IKEA, boxes left behind to accommodate me. No bumpy rides down steps or police Alfas in pursuit, but this is the authentic Mini-driving experience. You step-and-crouch down to get into the car, its floor so low-slung that you instinctively lift your feet over speed-bumps and check your heels to see if they are getting road-scraped. It all comes back: the extraordinary roominess, the gearstick like a wizard's wand topped with a bobble, the super-simple dash-board with its solitary dial and four switches. The steering wheel so big that you want to swivel it like a lifeboat coxswain. The hum. The vibration. The roar ...

'The sheer *noise*,' says Graham with a contented grin, as the Mini clears its throat and swings out on to the Leeds Road, making barking noises as I work up the gears. 'It's so deafening that you can't hear the click-click-click when you forget to cancel the indicator, like you've just done.' This accounts for the second most common sentence heard when the Beans go motoring, after Graham's all-purpose catch-phrase, 'No drama.' It's: 'You've left the indicator on,' yelled above the roar of the engine. Third comes 'Not again', as you turn on the wipers instead of the indicators, excusably since for reasons forgotten this particular Mini has the levers on the 'wrong' sides, compared with standard models.

That's another Mini thing. 'No two are the same,' says Graham, with feeling. Almost all of them have wipers with minds of their own, though, including the Beans'. As we crack along towards Huddersfield at a handsome 40mph, they stop and start on an inexplicable timetable. The barking gets louder. Maybe it's more to do with the brakes.

Is that petrol you can smell? Yes. Is that the road you can see skimming past through a hole in the floor? It is. Are people stopping, smiling and giving us a wave? They are. This is like driving an antique, except that you could buy one brand new as recently as 2000. Families such as the Beans use their Mini for day-to-day driving too. They're not yet collectors' cars, polished and garaged during the week and taken out for club meets at weekends.

They were never made to last. In the spirit of the 1960s the Mini was a use-and-throwaway accessory, a rust-bucket in the making. You hardly ever see one dozing quietly in the corner of a farmyard like a Morris Minor, awaiting the Second Coming of an enthusiast. For a car which was in production as recently as 2000, they are rare on the roads these days. But their design *did* last: it went on, largely unchanged, for decade after decade. I had a drink in the summer of 2009 with Robin Wight, the London adman who has the account of BMW, makers of the highly successful new MINI, and he made an interesting point. 'If the Mini had changed every decade, as nearly all cars do, the MINI is what it would have gradually become,' he said. 'But because it was such a great design, it stayed the same until – tada! – forty years of change happened all in one go.' As we shall see later on, that is precisely how the MINI's creators worked.

The original Mini bears out the well-known assertion that function is all, in design. Sometimes the theory overlooks the value of beauty and ornament, but not in this case. The car's simplicity of shape, fittings, instruments and driving is a *tour de force*. That is why it stayed in production with scarcely any change, except beneath the bonnet, for forty-two years. It has always been endearing, in the manner of all small, slightly rounded cars with smiley radiator grilles, and that increases as the years add to its 'classic' status. But it also revolutionised the design of small cars overnight. In 1999, it was voted second only to the Model T Ford, out of 700 entrants in a global contest which climaxed in Las Vegas, as the most significant car of the twentieth century – or, in a word, ever. It was a metal box on wheels which did the job and never suggested that its owners were putting on airs; but it was an outstandingly clever one.

That was due to its mastermind, Alec Issigonis, one of the brightest of the bright lights of the Levantine diaspora, families of Greek, Italian and other Mediterranean origin who were expelled or fled from what is now Turkey after the collapse of the cosmopolitan Ottoman Empire. He had three characteristics which were honed on the Morris Minor, largely but not entirely his work, and came to fruition in the Mini. They were all unusual, and as a trio exceptionally so.

First, he was worldly in his outlook. The child of a Levantine Greek father and a German mother, he was brought up in Smyrna, now Izmir, and played with the children of local Turks. He was rapaciously interested in car design and innovation across the world and copied or adapted it without hesitation. The Minor's shape owed much to American styling; the Mini's revolutionary engineering had antecedents in Germany and France. At the same time, his second distinction was to be British in the exaggerated way of many immigrants and the expats with whom his family mixed in Smyrna: 'more British than the British', down to affectations such as doing the *Daily Telegraph* crossword every day all his life without fail and insisting that no foods were better than marmalade and steak-and-kidney pie. When a relative brought houmous and kebabs to celebrate VE Day they were strictly kept for the family only. On top of this, Issigonis actually was a British citizen by birth; his paternal grandfather Demosthenes had been naturalised in Smyrna in exchange for helping Queen Victoria's Empire with a railway deal.

Demosthenes Issigonis studied in Manchester and admired the British, but he accepted the offer only as a safety net for troubled times. That was far-sighted; in due course it may be said to have saved his grandson's life. The Levantines were always potential outsiders, even under the Ottomans. They became actual outsiders following Greece's attempt to regain its ancient lands in Turkey at the end of the First World War. The Issigonises were among a handful of British citizens who were evacuated from Smyrna in 1922 just before the Turkish counter-attack swept vengefully into the city. They watched their neighbourhood burn from the safety of a Royal Navy destroyer.

This had a bearing on Alec Issigonis' third unusual characteristic, the lonely austerity which is especially reflected in his car design. His father Constantine, whose prosperous marine-engineering factory was destroyed along with the family mansion, died in despair at a transit camp in Malta on the way to England. Issigonis' life changed from one of privilege to counting the pennies in a London suburb. Instead of going to Oundle public school and Oxbridge, as originally planned, he enrolled at Battersea technical school and failed his maths exam three times. Thank goodness, so far as the future of cars was concerned, because his focus became engineering as a result; and 'focus' is the right word in the most intense sense. Issigonis was clubbable and a marvellous uncle to his sister's children and those of many of his friends, but he lived for cars. He never married and cared devotedly for his mother until she died in her eighties; together with his mannered style and choice of celebrity friends, such as Noël Coward, this led to rumours that he was gay. No one knows, but there is no evidence of active sexual liaisons and the wisest verdict is probably that of his great ally in the success of the Mini, John Cooper: 'He was married to motor cars. His whole life was motor cars. Day and night he'd talk about motor cars. He didn't talk about other things.'

All these talents made the Mini. But once it was created, Issigonis lost control of it. In accordance with his theories, it was launched as a masterpiece of simple, pared-down 'people's motoring' in the aftermath of Suez and petrol rationing. It rapidly became a racing car, a rally car, a celebrity accessory, an essential feature on the cover of *Time* magazine's special issue about Swinging London, complete with a member of the House of Lords at the wheel and his Lady crammed in the back. In no time, the little cars were regarded as just like little people, in Christine Perry's phrase. Half a century later, that is just how the Beans, my friends on the IKEA job, see theirs.

Merlin inherited his name from the family's previous pet, a budgie which took it in turn from the emblem of 15th Brigade, the Royal Engineers, the outfit which took Graham Bean to Iraq. The car has been part of the family from way back. Pooling memories, the Beans sort out its history – typical of 55,000 still registered in the UK – as we head for an evening drink with Leeds Mini Owners Club. 'We were just too fond of it to let it go,' muses Graham as Nicola unpicks the genealogy: 'It was my uncle's auntie's Mini, then he sort-of inherited it, did it up and passed it on to a cousin.' She was twenty-two and a lively girl who crashed it, but luckily not badly. David recalls: 'She was OK but she took out somebody's fence.' The crumpled car then came the Beans' way, with David in mind because he had just passed his driving test. They got it going again, but a much more comfy, secondhand Corsa came up, so the Mini ended up mothballed for nine years in his granny's garage. When she died, it was crunch time.

'Were we to sell it or do it up?' recalls Graham, a dilemma faced endlessly by affectionate owners of Minis, and resolved in the usual way. 'We couldn't bear the idea that it would probably be scrapped, and restoration was only going to cost a few grand. So we took it on a trailer to Newcastle where a friend has a garage specialising in Minis and over nine months he gradually restored it. He'd take photos and email them as he went along. We'd send him tyres and wheel arches every so often, that sort of thing. Modern Merlin was the result.'

He was ready in time for the London–Brighton 'Palace to

Pier' run, which the Beans entered with 2,200 other Mini owners. 'We went down to London, all of us, wondering if we'd get there,' says Graham. 'It was our first real outing in the car; the noise was deafening, there was no dashboard or seat padding. It was like being in a go-kart with a roof. You felt very tiny when you were overtaken by a big lorry. But you didn't feel unsafe. Size and vulnerability mean you're not complacent. You have to drive better.' Like the *expedit* power to cram in shopping, this is another reason why twenty-first century drivers stick so loyally to a mid-twentieth century design.

It was a cardinal point for Issigonis, repeated with increasing asperity as health and safety regulations gradually enmeshed the little car. 'The more uncomfortable you are, the better you will drive,' he declared, although it has never been clear why passengers should suffer as well. Nicola Bean isn't the only Mini user to unfold herself from the back seat with a grimace. When I tried sitting in the back for a bumpy spell round the suburbs of Morley, I ended up with a crease from the flimsily upholstered bench-back branded across my spine.

But the driving point stands. Minis need constant watchfulness through those big wide windows and both hands firmly on the wheel. I could never afford one when I wanted it. Insurance was a dead-end even with kindly parents who were prepared to risk my driving against their own no-claims bonuses. They looked at (a) a Mini and (b) an articulated lorry on the M1 and said: 'No, that isn't the car for you.' The nearest I got was a summer of lifts in a red one with a girl of unmistakable affluence called Caroline.

It was different for my older son Tom, who passed his driving test in 1999 and decided that getting between home and school, several times a day because of the endless 'study periods' in his A-level year, would be a lot easier if he had wheels. My wife Penny and I had already noticed that his generation listened to a lot of Sixties music and treated it with respect, unlike most other relics from that era. We now discovered the nostalgic, retro power of the Mini, because that was the car Tom wanted most. 'If you weren't a car enthusiast, there weren't many you'd heard of,' he remembers now. 'But the Mini was certainly one.' The Beetle was another, and after that affordable cars for newly licensed teenagers dwindled into battered old Fiestas or Peugeot 205s on the edge of failing their MoT.

The Mini had kept its cool to an impressive extent. It surely can't be fashionable to want the car your teacher drives, but Jon Cresswell, head of the sixth form at the boys' comprehensive, had a laid-back but inquiring and encouraging manner which appealed to the kids. He was also one of those men approaching middle age who have had Minis for ages and don't want to give them up. 'It was the only time in my life when I could even remotely be seen as a style icon,' he says today. The students were not quite so convinced. They used to watch as the Cresswell Mini negotiated the speed bumps to the school car park, and wonder why the top of his head wasn't flattened by the impacts.

Tom also had the example of one of his uncles, Penny's

brother Tony Cartledge, who was in the right place at the right time when famous or wealthy people wanted flowers and glowing psychedelic patterns painted on their souped-up Mini Coopers. A student at Kingston College of Art in the mid-1960s, Tony was commissioned by the son of a Conservative MP to paint a classic Sixties composition on his previously routine-looking saloon for £50. The car lived in Chelsea, always fashionable but then at the centre of the King's Road-Chelsea Girl whirl created by Mary Quant – an early and devoted Mini owner – with her King's Road boutique Bazaar and its many imitators. The commission went well; a photograph even appeared in the *Daily Express* with Tony's girlfriend draped in the then traditional way on the bonnet. 'But the next day I took the car round,' he recalls, 'and although the morning was nearing its end, he appeared at the front door in a silken Paisley dressing gown. He bade me wait awhile, while he dug out not his money, but his mummy. She sniffily looked me up and down, then declared that £50 was "far too much" and handed me £30. I was bloody choked, but could do nothing about it.' Another young member of the commissioning family later became a prominent Conservative under Margaret Thatcher, maybe impressed by this lesson in hard-nosed home economics.

Our Tom also had a tight budget. He briefly looked at a secondhand Vauxhall Nova pimped out with sporty racing seats, but prudently decided that anything too nice would be unwise, because of the risk of scrapes, bumps and family clumsiness. One of us duly proved him right with the Mini, by falling into the old trap of flipping up the front passenger seat with the door open, then shutting the door and yanking the seat back down, a sequence which in Issigonis' miracle of small space can, and in this case did, crush the plastic side-pocket.

So a Mini it was. There was a small ad in the *Yorkshire Evening Post* and soon afterwards Tom was driving a black Mini Mayfair back from Jean Barrass's home in Garforth on the other side of Leeds. It had been in the paper's Car of the Week section and the £1,750 which Mrs Barrass was asking seemed a fair price. Its previous owners had been a Miss Kirkman and Mrs Blackland, both of Harrogate, who didn't sound like speed demons who would have hammered the engine. Mrs Barrass talked as fondly as the Beans about how the car had been one of the family and how much she would miss it. It was going to be part of our family now.

'I would have preferred red,' Tom admitted later, but you can't have everything. (His granny, who had bought a keyring with a miniature red Mini on it, quickly painted that black.) It looked like a tiny London taxi. The interior of the car was also quite smart, with silvery-grey fake velour coverings on the seats, and the handy father of one of Tom's friends fitted a pair of speakers on the back shelf, plus a spaghetti of wires by the front passenger's feet which added an authentically funky Sixties feel.

The Mini proved a sturdy little commuter. Even when Tom overloaded it with friends and it died on the final hill to the school, there were enough of them to scramble out and push to get it going again. Some of them were doing physics A-level and they worked out that the passenger load had tilted the remaining petrol in the car's almost-empty fuel tank beyond the reach of the pump. Like a calmer version of the final scene in *The Italian Job,* that great epic of Mini glory, they calculated how many could get back in without the same thing happening again.

The car also disappeared in a cloud of steam on the way home from a lecture at Leeds University by Ed Balls, then an adviser to the Chancellor of the Exchequer, Gordon Brown. Another handy Dad took a look when the party limped back, with the engine sounding on the verge of death. 'There's no water in the radiator,' he said in the time-honoured, patient way of parents explaining mechanical basics to novice offspring drivers, before lending Tom a tin of sealant.

The Mayfair had a curious distinction, which appealed to us all, of being able to run on both leaded and unleaded petrol, an attribute singular to that particular model and only for a couple of years. Tom was also fond of the windscreen wipers, which were tiny and had three speeds: slow, medium and manic. He was slight himself and the general mini-ness of everything made him feel at home. He got clubbishly flashed by other Minis, and drivers in general treated the unthreatening little car with kindness. The Mini's very size and vulnerability were real aids to careful driving, he reckoned, just as Graham Bean does. 'Going faster than 40mph felt terrifying, and the time we reached 60mph on a dual carriageway wasn't something you'd ever forget,' Tom recalls. 'You never wanted to break any speed limits in the Mini.' He had taken his driving test in one, in circumstances which added to his caution: his examiner was being examined by an examiner of examiners from the Department of

Transport. Given the cosy space inside a Mini, for all Sir Alec Issigonis' wizardry in enlarging it, Tom had to ask the examiner of examiners to move and duck down whenever he needed to go backwards, and particularly in the test's notorious section on reversing round a corner.

Still more dramatic evidence of the Mini's vulnerability and need for intense concentration at the wheel was given to me by Tom's prospective mother-in-law, Radha Dharmaratnam, as we all prepared for his wedding to her daughter Abi in September 2009. Radha and her husband Suri are both doctors, originally from Sri Lanka where they had travelled around in a dignified way in a Morris Oxford. But one of their friends there drove an orange Mini Cooper and in Colombo, as in London, the marque was cool. When they moved to Britain in the 1980s, they went to see a Mini for sale in a village near Norwich where they were first based. Radha got in, pressed some buttons and pedals and the car started rolling down the drive. Like the Beans' young cousin, she nearly took out the owner's fence. 'Luckily I found the brake and jammed it down,' she remembered. 'I stopped just short.'

This was the beginning of an exciting time for the car, which took Radha to work in King's Lynn every morning. She has a sense of dash, nowadays expressed in an open-top Mercedes, and she enjoyed getting the best out of the Mini, even though it was a basic and not terribly high-powered model with automatic gears, which the shaken fence-owner parted with for £200.

'I remember taking it for a proper drive for the first time and rounding a corner and thinking, "This is so *low*,"' she says, lighting on an Issigonis inspiration. The relative broadness of the car, with its ten-inch wheels as far out on each corner as they can be fitted, gives an exceptionally low centre of gravity. From that come the stability and roadholding which helped Paddy Hopkirk, Rauno Aaltonen and Timo Makinen to triumph in the Monte Carlo rallies between 1964 and '67. Radha was a bit of a Pat Moss herself and remembers braking unintentionally hard on black ice in Norwich and spinning 180 degrees, so that she was facing back the way she had come. 'We stayed upright,' she says, still with satisfaction after all these years. And apart from not hitting anything, staying upright was what mattered.

Radha never did hit anything, but she had a real Mini adventure when her car was picked up inadvertently by a lorry as both of them sped along the dual carriageway to King's Lynn at around 5.30 one dark morning. 'I don't know how it happened, but I was sort of hooked by the lorry under the bumper or my front wing,' she recalls. 'I suddenly realised that I was being dragged along. It was terrifying. I didn't know what to do and the lorry didn't seem to have noticed.' Her story struck echoes with me, after a similar episode on the busy three lanes of Cromwell Road in West London, when a truck and I clashed side on, and my parents' Triumph Herald, which I had borrowed to shift stuff down to my London flat, was left with three dramatic circular wheel-hub impressions on its door panels: it looked like an Etch-a-Sketch. The truck driver never knew, any more than Radha's did, even when she took desperate measures at the roundabout where she had to turn off for King's Lynn.

'I just turned the steering wheel left as hard as I could and there was a dreadful creaking noise. The Mini and I went left, and the bumper and part of the offside wing went on, still hooked to the lorry.' They probably fell off soon afterwards but if not, and if there is a Norfolk lorry driver still wondering how he arrived at his depot with part of a Mini attached to his wagon like fishbait, then that is the reason. But the spell of super-concentrated, Issigonis-style driving *had* got Radha and the Mini free. They limped on to work and Radha and Suri eventually got the wing fixed, although its handsome British racing green still hadn't been repainted when they moved to Bury in Lancashire with their two-year-old daughter.

Abi now enters the story in her own right, pictured in a family photograph in her Bugs Bunny sweater with the wounded Mini in the background. The photo was taken shortly before an expedition famous in Dharmaratnam folklore, when Suri and Radha took Abi to Bolton to buy her very first bike. As befits a small girl, this was bright pink with stabilisers, and Abi fell in love with it with such a passion that, once sat on it and gripping the handlebars in excitement, she would not let go or get off. 'We tried to tell her and persuade her and tempt her but she wouldn't budge,' says Suri, whose own speciality, which I share and which has led us both to make the acquaintance of a number of AA patrol men, was running the petrol tank as low as possible before refilling. So in the end, in another demonstration of Issigonis' extraordinarily accommodating interior, small girl seated on small bike was loaded in exactly as she was. The front wheel was wedged between the Mini's front seats with the back in the rear seat well. And thus the Dharmaratnams travelled home to Bury.

Back in the Beans' car, I am now squashed in the back, pink if not bicycle-shaped, and rummaging inquisitively in the big door pockets which Issigonis claimed were designed to hold bottles for his favourite gin Martinis. Graham and Michèle have a bottle too, but it is of Castrol lead additive, which they have to mix with the petrol every time they fill the small, 25-litre tank. Driving a classic Mini these days involves a round of adjustments and tinkerings like this; luckily Michèle works in accounts at a big motoring store, so supplies are handy if the bottle starts to run out. And Merlin gives a useful 50mpg in return.

Such complications don't put the Beans off using the car daily. Merlin usually drops Nicola at high school in Cleckheaton, where another family's classic Mini keeps it company in the car park. Like our Tom, she thinks that Minis are cool. 'Everyone knows about them,' she says. 'Loads of dads and uncles have had them, and they keep showing *The Italian Job* on TV.' Teenagers have enlisted in the endless discussions about glitches and hidden references in the film, which have been reinvigorated by online chatrooms. David chips in: 'I was reading in *Nuts* the other day that when one of the Minis goes over the cliff it's red as it goes over, then blue on the way down.' Everybody aaahs and mmmmms, deeply intrigued. We start chatting about Jeremy Clarkson's plan to restage the film's sewer chase, this time in Ireland rather than Coventry, which stood in for

Italy in 1969. Then the talk turns to the maximum speed anyone has got out of Merlin. 'Wasn't it seventy on the M1?' There's even a suggestion of tipping seventy-five on a local 'mad mile'. A Leeds club member is said to have done 105 in his, though that was an ultra-customised version.

The tiger under the little bonnet, so much a part of Mini lore, even features in shopping chat, to which we return as Merlin pootles us home. In another of their own versions of *The Italian Job*, the Beans can slip between the bollards in Tesco's car park. Like Michael Caine's gold bullion in the film, their weekly shopping bags meanwhile fill the whole of the back seat. 'Obviously I can't use the boot,' says Michèle, making an assumption common to all Mini owners who know how tiny the supposed main luggage space is. The Beans' is already filled with the spare wheel, battery and a trolley jack, for quick and easy puncture repairs. Merlin doesn't have the early Issigonis attempt to improve matters: Mini boots were initially designed to stay open if necessary, with luggage strapped on top as in an old-fashioned touring car, and the rear number-plate hinged to dangle down below and still be visible.

So are we heading for a cliff to dangle down ourselves, until one of us does a Michael Caine impression and says, 'Hang on a minute, lads (and lassies), I've got an idea'? No. The Beans have got work to do and I want to find out how all this happened. Where did this wonderful car come from? How – apart from stamping down on that strange little starter-button on the floor – did it start?

## Chapter Two
# Born from a Bubble

*'This is it. I want it in production in twelve months.'*
*Sir Leonard Lord, chairman of BMC, July 1958*

THE STORY OF THE MINI BEGINS with bubble cars, weird contraptions like the one which regularly had my brother and me on its tail, spitting lead from imaginary wing-mounted machine-guns as we swooped down Tinshill Road in Leeds. That was 1956 and English boys knew what to do to anything called Heinkel or Messerschmidt. Along with our best friend Carl Wood we dived out of the sun shouting 'Angels 1-0-5' and similar battle cries from War Picture Library's sixpenny weeklies. The bubble car's friendly owner, Mr Atkinson from across the road, knew the rules of the game and fired back, squinting along his index and middle fingers. He also knew that he could drive faster than we could run – although not by a lot.

Similar scenes were being played out across Britain at the time, as freedom from rationing and austerity turned people's attention to more prosperous notions. Foremost among these was TV – our gang met at the Luya family's because they had one of the road's only sets and their children were allowed to watch ITV rather than just the BBC. But greater in wonder even than the telly was the dream of personal transport. There had been motorbikes for ages and the more prosperous of our family's friends had Morris Minors and in one case even a stately Humber. But Mr Atkinson was a Tinshill Road pioneer of something much cheaper, which was also stylish and natty in spite of its Luftwaffe name.

Nipping about in his bubble car, he was part of a romantic tradition which appropriately had other aircraft connections. Late in 2008, I helped my photographer colleague Denis Thorpe with an exhibition he was organising at the Lowry Centre on Salford Quays, of a century of *Guardian* photography by staff based in Manchester. The earliest of them, Walter Doughty, had a particular interest in aircraft; his heyday coincided with their pioneering days, and he went up at air displays with the original, magnificent men in their flying machines. On a quiet evening when he was waiting in London for the Prime Minister, Stanley Baldwin, to emerge from Downing Street, he caught the sinister outline of a German Zeppelin as it drifted overhead.

To give context to these pictures, Denis and I leafed through archive issues of the then *Manchester Guardian* and found a fascinating selection of 'flying craze' offers, which between 1905 and 1914 took up more than a quarter of the classified advertising. You could build your own plane for £100 (£8,000 today), there were unflattering undergarments for keeping warm in an open cockpit and all manner of stylish helmets. It was a blueprint for a world such as the one conjured up by Stella Gibbons in *Cold Comfort Farm*, whose heroine Flora Poste and her modish friends dart about the country in their own small aircraft.

Cost and other practicalities meant that this delightful prospect remained fiction, but the bubble cars of the early 1950s were an earthbound version of the dream. The parallels were particularly close in the case of Mr Atkinson, who had served in wartime aircrews and was tickled that his bubble was a Messerschmidt Kabinenroller. When he occasionally allowed us to sit behind him in the passenger seat, it was exactly how we imagined being the navigator in the cockpit of a wartime Messerschmidt fighter plane and, indeed, that is what the Kabinen part of the Kabinenroller was. '*Achtung Spitfeuer!*' The Messerschmidt company was banned from making aircraft after the Second World War but they ingeniously grafted a version of their notorious Me109's cockpit, for which they had hundreds of machine tools set up, on to a three-wheeled invalid-carriage frame. It was an odd but workable marriage. Mr and Mrs Atkinson could get to picnics at Bolton Abbey much more quickly than the rest of us, who were forced to change buses or trains at Skipton.

The Messerschmidt and the Heinkel were the best-known bubbles, thanks to their notorious names, but they had plenty of rivals, all eager to serve the infant market of returning prosperity. They were round, elliptical, dart-shaped or like rollerskating eggs, glorified motorbikes in a way, but there was also plenty of serious and imaginative engineering involved. To sense its extent, simply pay a visit to the National Bubble Car Museum in Lincolnshire, a warehouse of metal, wood and fibreglass fixed in gloopy shapes like those children's book characters, the Barbapapa Family. Mike and Paula Cooper who run the place, after an apprenticeship tarting up Citroen 2CVs in Frome, leave you in no doubt that the little cars had the potential to go far.

'Yes, it's basically a tin box with go-kart steering,' Mike admitted, running a loving hand along a pale blue Kabinenroller. 'But goodness, it's clever. Just three bolts fix the scooter-size engine to the body, the brakes are simple cables like a pedal-bike's, and look at this neat arrangement in the back. Old Messerschmidt gave you a seat-and-a-half there.' He flipped up a child-sized side section of the tiny bench to show how the Germans made room for a modest suitcase (a detail the Mini was later to copy) if the bubble was out for a spin with just two adults inside. 'Strictly speaking, it's a three-seater,' Mike said. 'The design is brilliantly simple, and all done as cheaply as possible.'

There were disadvantages, of course, which help to explain why the bubbles never really took off. It was just as well that Mr Atkinson's Messerschmidt couldn't get airborne, because to go into reverse you had to stop the engine to change gear and then start up again. Other bubbles dispensed with reverse altogether; they were small enough to manoeuvre almost anywhere by going forwards and doing the tightest of U-turns, or light enough for their users to manhandle them to face the other way. But you don't reach a mass market with cars like that.

The Coopers had always been interested in small, clever

cars. Paula started as a mechanic at the age of three; her father was an engineer who brought his work home as a hobby and taught her the first sentence she ever spoke: 'Hold this spanner, would you?' Their Citroens in Somerset had the austere simplicity common to most of the bubbles and the Mini. 'A child could take the 2CV apart,' says Paula. 'We'd dismantle them completely in twenty minutes. When a customer came in with a rusted chassis, we'd send them off to do the Frome Town Walk [an hour's historical stroll] and have lunch at a pub. When they got back, their car was fixed up and back together again.'

Their own 2CV Hissing Sid – because of the noise of its air-cooler – took them to France regularly, and it was on one of these journeys that they started discussing bubble cars. France had a feisty tradition of them, including another egg on wheels, the Mathis, whose disproportionately large 707cc engine so alarmed the French government that they withdrew the vehicle's road licence. The Paris sculptor Paul Arzens designed another model which he actually called L'Oeuf, capable of 37mph and with only one pedal, which doubled through highly skilled mechanics as both accelerator and brake.

Natural enthusiasts, the Coopers became more and more diverted by the sheer engineering élan of these micro-vehicles. They dissected a German model, ironically called the Goliath; then an Italian Bambi, only 94 inches long and more like a dodgem than a real car. Britain came up with a Frisky, a Petite and a Bamby with a 'y', a single-seater aimed at the cheapest motorbike licence category which was made

in Hull by an engineer called Alan Hall, in secretive circumstances. 'Alan never would tell us how many were made,'
said Mike reflectively, stroking the museum's fine example,
number A768 NKH, which was the first off the production
line. 'But we've worked out from the chassis numbers that
it wouldn't have been more than twenty. It's basically a
covered moped, and that's the point about bubble cars.
Their job was to carry people about fairly quickly and –
crucially – keep them dry, with just a modicum of comfort.'
He could have been Sir Alec Issigonis speaking about the
extreme austerity of the first Minis (although, as we will
discover, these were anything but dry).

The process led inevitably to the National Bubble Car
Museum, particularly after plans for something similar by
RUM, the Register of Unusual Microcars, never got beyond
what Mike recalls as 'a rather depressing newsletter which
ran articles such as "Can anyone donate floorpaint?"' The
couple's first simple building near RAF Cranwell grew and
grew as they collected bubbles or came to the attention of
recent widows of enthusiasts who had been left with an
elderly Heinkel or Gogomobil and didn't know what to do
with it.

You could linger for many happy hours among the weird
contraptions, many of them considerably bigger than a Mini
(overall; never remotely in terms of interior space). Who
wouldn't have been just a little tempted in the 1950s by the
Berkeley, a stylish three-wheeler like a baby E-type Jaguar,
albeit made in Biggleswade by Britain's largest caravan
company? Or the 1949 Bond, marvellously handsome in

beige carriagework and with a novel steering system which attached the engine to the front wheels and turned the whole thing on a worm and screw system of super-low gears? It was actually called the Minicar, the first motor-trade use of the name which was to become so hugely famous. And its creator, Lawrie Bond, was a sparky, ingenious inventor who could well have been another Issigonis.

The son of an artist and slightly obsessive local historian in Preston, Bond showed an early knack for mechanical invention, playing with miniature steam engines and Meccano and poring over exploded diagrams of engines in the *Boy's Own Paper*. He left school at sixteen to start paid work as an apprentice at a steam-powered lorry company in 1923, but soon transferred to aeroplanes. He started his own light-aircraft manufacturing company and by the end of the Second World War had thirty staff. Peacetime's abrupt end to RAF repair contracts turned his attention to another high-speed market: he started building lightweight racing cars.

The first was a 500cc hill-climber called the Doodlebug, which *Autocar* magazine described enthusiastically as a 'jet-propelled yellow slug'. Speed and lightness were his Holy Grails; the heaviest thing in the Doodlebug was himself, wrapped in a driving helmet like an RAF pilot, complete with beaky nose and military moustache sticking out at the front. The car was so nimbly weightless that it had to carry bags of wet sand as ballast when racing, while its engine drove the wheels at such speed that Bond had to glue the tyres to the wheel-rims to stop them slipping off. Inevitably, he came to grief in a Doodlebug, crashing at speed and breaking his jaw and several front teeth. But that merely drove him on.

Still wearing his bandages, he went back to his factory in Blackpool (which is still there, albeit in a different role as the local Labour Party headquarters) and immersed himself in adapting the Doodlebug for conventional drivers on ordinary roads. The Minicar went through seven, increasingly sophisticated, models and also developed a small family – the Minitruck, Minivan, Shopper and ambitiously named Family Safety Saloon, which had two hammocks in the back for child passengers. Bond's wife, a former journalist with a lively pen, promoted the range with vim: why wait forever for a conventional saloon, when 60 per cent of mainstream car production was reserved by Government edict for export? Why spend a fortune on petrol, when a Bond could do 104mpg? Why pay Britain's punitive purchase tax, which added 66 per cent to the cost of an ordinary car? The Bond Minirange all evaded it, because they were so small and relatively low-powered.

It almost worked. Pauline Bond's contacts won an endorsement from Stirling Moss, Britain's most celebrated racing driver at the time, even though the Minicar's top speed was only 40mph. This was backed by a series of plucky achievements, forerunners of the dramatic events which were later to make the real Mini's name. In 1954, a Minicar unofficially entered the Monte Carlo Rally, skimming like an insect over snow-choked roads which trapped heavier rivals. It registered an official 63mpg average for the taxing event. Bond enthusiasts vied to make journeys such as London to Geneva or a 9000-mile tour of Europe which became regular David and Goliath features of motoring magazines. The company cheekily produced a £4 16s 4d (£98 today) Continental touring kit, angling headlight beams to the right and the like, and hinted at triumphs in the narrow lanes and maze-like alleys of mainland Europe by reminding readers of advertisements that a Bond was the Only Car in the World Which Can Turn Round In Its Own Length. The market reacted. A friend of mine, Audrey Burnley, remembers her father buying a Minicar and hurtling the family in it through the Yorkshire Dales, targeting much bigger Fords and sometimes overtaking them, with a mixture of cunning and the Bond's sudden, slender manoeuvrability.

Bubble cars never sold in serious numbers, but the Bond Minicar did. More than 26,500 were made and in 1956 it suddenly looked as though they might make it into the real big time. In July that year, after months of threats, President Gamal Abdul Nasser of Egypt nationalised the Suez canal and there was a panic in Britain which is hard to imagine nowadays. Petrol prices went through the roof, and when they peaked in December at 3s 6d a gallon rationing was reintroduced. It had been lifted only two years earlier after fifteen years of restrictions, starting with the outbreak of the Second World War in 1939. The mood in 1956 was reminiscent of that earlier grim time. Nasser blocked the canal with scuttled ships while his Arab allies cut off pipelines which supplied a fifth of the United Kingdom's oil. The British Motor Corporation sacked six thousand workers without notice.

With hindsight, it was all a hiccough economically. Britain's imperial reputation was changed for good by Suez; the damage to her prosperity lasted only briefly. The BMC workers were soon back on the assembly lines and the cars rolling off them again. But the scare held for long enough to trigger a hugely significant change of direction at the company, and it was one that led directly to the Mini.

For two years prior to Suez, there was a period of complacency and torpor in British car-making. The Morris Minor, the most exciting product technically, was already nearly eight years old. The dominant British Motor Corporation was an unhappy marriage between the former fierce rivals Morris and Austin, made in 1952 for good commercial reasons but with little enthusiasm on either side. Staff at both companies were often long in the tooth and unable to forget their past differences. The end to duplication which was supposed to follow the merger never happened. Instead major lines such as the Minor and the Austin A35 sold cosily in an easy, protected domestic market whose buyers were eager for any set of wheels now that the Government's compulsory quotas for export had been lifted. 'Most of our people have never had it so good,' said the Prime Minister Harold Macmillan in 1957. The carmakers had seldom had it so cushy.

The sense of inertia struck outsiders and they began to comment on it, increasingly embarrassingly. Lawrence Pomeroy of *The Motor* buttonholed Lord at the Earls Court Motor Show in 1955 and told him that it was high time BMC 'progressed from cart springs and built something a little more interesting'. Things came to a head the same year when the Duke of Edinburgh visited Longbridge. Inspecting some sketchy new designs shown him by Lord, he commented, with his trademark tartness, 'Sir Leonard, I think you should have another look at things because I'm not sure these are up to the foreign competition.' Some of those present thought that he was riled because Lord had joshed him clumsily about the fact that he drove a Land Rover instead of Austin's peculiar rival, the Champ, which could throw its entire gear ratio into reverse so that British troops using it in Malaya could zoom backwards out of ambushes at five different speeds. But the royal jibe hit home.

It had an immediate effect. Lord commissioned new designers to look at most of BMC's ageing fleet, among them the highly rated Pininfarina specialists from Italy, where Fiat's new cars were making news. His thoughts had also already turned to bringing back prominent members of past Austin or Morris teams who had shown talent. Like Chairman Mao in China, he decided on a Great Leap Forward, basing his strategy on three new, linked models, big, medium and small like the Three Bears. One name stood out on his list: Alec Issigonis, the man primarily responsible for the Morris Minor, which was an immediate success on its launch in 1948, and remained BMC's best-selling car.

For most of their careers, the two men had been on opposite sides of the great divide in the British car industry – Austin versus Morris – which had ended with the merger into BMC. Lord was an aggressive and chippy businessman who had risen from the shopfloor. Brought up in the Hare and Hounds in Coventry where his father was landlord, he was asked by one of his early employers what his ambitions were, and replied: 'To sit in your chair.' He went much further than that; spotted and promoted by William Morris, the future Lord Nuffield, he was managing director of Morris Motors by the age of thirty-nine and made a huge success of the job. But then his headstrong side took over and the two men fell out. It may have been over money; it may have been that he refused to end a secret affair with a Cowley factory secretary which had reached the ears of an outraged Lady Nuffield. At all events, he resigned in 1939 and took a similar job at the enemy, Austin, promising that he would 'tear Cowley apart brick by bloody brick'. In a metaphorical sense he was to do so; he led for Austin during the BMC merger, and once he was in charge of the new company Austin men and Austin interests came first.

Issigonis was by contrast a Morris man. He had built his reputation with a series of highly inventive vehicles during the Second World War, most of them destined to remain as experiments or prototypes but with engineering insights which senior managers including the chief executive Sir Miles Thomas noticed and admired. When the company finally decided to make a replacement for the sturdy but ageing Morris 8 after the Second World War, Issigonis was chosen to lead the design team. Project Mosquito, as it was called, became the Morris Minor, and although Issigonis had colleagues whose influence on the car was crucial, his was the name which the Minor made. He left Morris in 1952 to design a luxury saloon for the small but upmarket carmakers Alvis, but their finances could not run to the brilliant but expensive prototype which he designed. So just as Lord began asking around, the man he particularly wanted to tempt to Longbridge was interested in finding a way back. His move to Alvis had conveniently removed him from the scene during the problems and nastiness of the BMC merger, and he soon agreed terms.

These gave him the right to choose his own team and to bring in some talented outsiders from his Alvis project as consultants. They arrived in December 1955 and plunged themselves into outline drawings and specifications for the middle car in the proposed range of three. It got a futuristic codename, XC001, and by late summer their experimental workshop was humming away in a single-storey brick block, unremarkable and deliberately isolated at the furthest western corner of the huge Longbridge site. Then Nasser struck, and the world was turned upside down

Issigonis was busy as ever, scribbling on his Arclight sketch pads, when a memo from Lord arrived. Would Issigonis come over and see him at the 'Kremlin', the management offices at Longbridge named for the chairman's tough and ruthless style? Spreading out sheets of data and newspaper stories on Suez and petrol rationing, Lord told Issigonis to shelve the big car and concentrate on the smallest of the planned range instead 'to drive all these bloody bubble cars off the road'. It was a kneejerk reaction to wild exaggeration. Media hype of the bubble effect and the little cars' odd and noticeable shapes had given the impression that their increase in popularity after Suez was much greater than it actually was. Only around 3000 were registered the following year, compared to 425,000 cars in Britain overall. But they included some potent examples of good engineering: Lawrie Bond's Minicars, for example, and the Isetta, made by that giant-in-the-making BMW under licence from Italy, where the Fiat 600, precursor of the Mini-sized Cinquecento, was also attracting international interest.

Lord was notorious for acting on hunches and often without consultation, but he was not stupid. He did not foresee a world of bubbles, or want to make BMC's own version of one. A year earlier, he had allowed the company's experimental workshop at Cowley to have a go at that and the resulting 'Morris Bubblecar' prototype exposed only the limitations of underpowered engines, not the merits of insect size. BMC's technical director Sidney Smith had shown Cowley's chief stylist, Sid Goble, a Gogomobil like the one in Mike and Paula Cooper's National Bubble Car Museum and said, 'That's the car of the future' – but he was talking about size, not power. Addressing the 1957 Motor Show's press dinner, Lord's deputy George Harriman amplified the point, arguing that the public wanted not bubble cars but small and low-priced real ones which were economical on fuel. If BMC could find a way of meeting that demand, they would do so.

So the die was cast, and in a way that exactly suited Issigonis' private plans. Ever since his first Morris Minor experiments at the end of the Second World War, he had been thinking about what he called a 'charwoman's car':

small and cheap but using ideas gleaned from his military experiments about compact engines, clever steering and suspension and lots of room in a small space. His head was so full of these ideals that he was able to give Lord the car's ten essential features at their meeting, on the spot. The chairman took them on board immediately and said: 'Go ahead and show us you can do it.' When Issigonis got back to the design office, his deputy Jack Daniels remembered, he was grinning from ear to ear.

The change of direction also chimed with Issigonis' whole career path, which paralleled Lawrie Bond's to a remarkable extent. When Bond was a boy reading the *Boy's Own Paper* in Lancashire, Issigonis was sharing his copy in Smyrna with his best friend Donald Riddle, whose father was an expat British businessman in the city. Issigonis' love of Meccano was even greater than Bond's. When his father made a potentially dangerous last visit to their house in 1922, with the Turkish army entering the suburbs of Izmir and order breaking down in all directions, young Alec begged Constantine Issigonis to let him go too, so that he could collect the models which he and Donald had made. His appeals were so passionate that his father agreed and the pair made the perilous journey from their evacuation warship in a hired launch, returning with the Meccano stashed in bags along with heirlooms his father rescued.

The postwar hill-climbs and sprints which saw Bond's Doodlebug zoom round the circuits were also a favourite of Issigonis. His Lightweight Special racer shared the Doodlebug's virtues of speed and lightness, to the extent that dozens of small holes were drilled in the metal body-work just to reduce its weight. Like Bond, with his RAF moustache and tally-ho style, Issigonis was also raring to take on anything German, and he encouraged colleagues to spit at Volkswagen Beetles, which had wiped out the Morris Minor in export sales to the United States. He needed no encouragement to denounce Heinkel and Messerschmidt bubble cars.

He was now the man charged with driving them into oblivion. Still heady with the chance to experiment which Alvis had given him, he accepted a deadline from Lord which was unprecedentedly tight. A trial version of the new 'baby car' had to be ready by mid-1957 and, provided that it proved acceptable, the real thing would start production in the late summer of 1958. Lord promised to place Longbridge's enormous resources at the project team's disposal and gave Issigonis an all-purpose docket allowing him to make use of any department he liked. Released from the moderating hand of senior colleagues, such as Reg Job and Vic Oak who had tempered his wilder ideas on the Morris Minor, he took full advantage of this. It was from this era that his old nicknames such as Ginigonis and Porkigonis, based on his strong views about food and drink and conservative diet, were joined by a new one, coined by disgruntled workers faced with imperious demands: Aragonis. Others grumbled, 'Issy-gone-yet?'

This autocracy too was to play a part in the Mini's design, for both good and ill. The concept would be clearer, purer and less of a compromise than the Morris Minor, but it would also be riddled with practical flaws. In his first stint with Morris Motors, Issigonis had benefited from a father-figure, the avuncular but steely chief executive Sir Miles Thomas. They met initially on a fire-watching stint during the Blitz, when mandarins such as Sir Miles would take their turn alongside assembly-line workers and junior design staff like Issigonis. A former journalist and stunt pilot, Thomas took a liking to the young man and had no doubt about his exceptional talents. But, like the father whom Issigonis had lost so young, he made his displeasure clear at any sign of arrogance towards colleagues. He would have been aghast at the change in his protégé during the creation of the Mini.

There are many accounts of Issigonis' behaviour during this time on the record; another, previously unpublished, was told me by a retired Cowley engineer, Malcolm Russell. An apprentice between 1953 and 1959 at Pressed Steel Fisher, which made car body shells for Morris just the other side of the Oxford ring road, he recalled, 'There was Alec in a meeting in our offices with our engineering director Jeff Robinson and the chief body engineer Ken Osborne. Over some technical point Ken said, "Well, Mr Issigonis, in my experience ..." But before he could continue, Issigonis interjected with, "Mr Osborne, in my experience you have no experience." How things proceeded from there one can only imagine, but this story ran around our office very quickly.'

The earlier, humbler Issigonis would perhaps have made progress with the Mini more smoothly, and in the process might have avoided some of the many glitches which were to damage the car's reputation almost fatally in the first months after its launch. But his colleagues recognised the excitement of what he was achieving and the inevitable stress involved; for the process which he set in train was hugely complicated, involving three revolutionary changes in car engineering.

Its starting point was as simple as could be: a quite exceptional reduction in size. Issigonis was famous for drawing sketches on napkins, tablecloths and even with chalk on various floors, but he never began with pretty views of the exterior. His first drawings were always of people in chairs with measurements scribbled around them. With ADO15, as the Mini project was initially called from the usual code of Austin Drawing Office, project 15, he then made the pictures real. He asked for a sheet of plywood and four Morris Minor seats to stand on it, plus volunteers to sit in them at various distances from one another in progressive states of discomfort or ease. As the experiment developed, he measured the whole 'box', preserving ample legspace but eventually getting its dimensions down to an astonishing ten feet long, four and a half feet wide and just under four and a half feet high. This was the Mini in virtual form, the original conception of the car's extraordinary compactness combined with roominess inside.

How did it happen? Through the first and most important of Issigonis' revolutions: front-wheel drive with the engine placed transverse or sideways across the car, sitting with its ends pointing at the two front wheels rather than fore-and-aft which was overwhelmingly the traditional system. The simple, ninety-degree turn brought the length of the engine compartment down to eighteen inches and created the car's 'miraculous' extra seating space. The idea was not new, but needed all manner of other adjustments to work, especially with front-wheel drive, which is what had put most other designers off. 'Most' is the accurate word, because there had been a very small number of experimental front-wheel drive, transverse-engined cars previously, and a few which never got beyond blueprints but were widely studied. Issigonis seldom admitted it, but his breakthroughs came after prolonged reflection on the experiments, drawings and writings of others.

In particular, his friend Lawrence Pomeroy had produced a meticulous design of a car with a transverse engine in *The Motor* as early as 1939, even calling the concept a Mini-Motor. It came to nothing, but, interestingly, 'Pom' (as everyone called him) was also asked by Sir Leonard Lord to come up with some anti-bubble car suggestions, and was actually working on them at the time of Lord's fateful meeting at the Kremlin with Issigonis. Pom's 'cart-spring' tease of Lord at the 1955 Motor Show led to this. 'Bloody well tell us what to build and we'll build it,' Lord exploded in reply, before paying Pomeroy for two years' research. The resulting 'Maximin' was a disappointment, with none of the brilliance of the Mini or indeed the Mini-Motor, and like the latter, it went nowhere.

Issigonis himself had experimented with a transverse engine in the Morris Minor, designing a front-wheel drive version shortly before he left for Alvis, which was completed as a test car by his colleagues at Cowley. It was still around in 1956 and played a small but helpful part in the necessary process of tactfully keeping senior management informed of the way that thinking on ADO15 was developing. Issigonis' stalwart deputy Jack Daniels had to drive over from Cowley soon after Lord's meeting with Issigionis, and the day had started with a heavy snowfall. The experimental Minor had the best road-holding qualities of any car in the factory pool, in his view, so he used it to commute. He also parked it deliberately by the Kremlin, where Lord and his deputy George Harriman duly noticed it, looked under the bonnet, and were interested and impressed. They recognised, as all car designers have done since, that Issigonis was pulling off that rare development, a turning point in motor mechanics; something so different and radical that a whole decade later the film *The Italian Job* could still pull off a visual quip by having a mechanic look for the workings at the rear of one of the heroic Mini Coopers. Transverse engines and front-wheel drive became the template for almost all small and medium-sized cars which followed the Mini. Only Ford held off for seventeen years until 1976, when the Fiesta became its first model to adopt the system.

But there was now a problem for Issigonis, small in size but crucial in effect. The shift in the engine position and the new car's tiny size placed an enormous strain on the universal joints, one of the cleverest of the many mechanical tricks which make cars work. The joints change the direction of rotary motion, allowing a driveshaft pointing from bonnet to boot to transmit power to axles running sideways between the wheels, a 'bending' of energy through up to ninety degrees. The angles and stresses of his transverse engine, front-wheel drive and independent suspension were such that conventional universal joints could not cope with the transfer of power without unacceptable strain. Dozens were tried and all cracked. Even while they lasted, they altered the car's handling and undid all the road-holding advantages of front-wheel drive.

No customer was going to buy that. But what was the answer? For all Issigonis' genius and knowledge, there seemed to be no joint which could link his brilliant engine adjustment to the driveline and the baby car's unprecedentedly small, ten-inch wheels. Almost at its outset, the revolutionary change was in danger of becoming a technological dead end. The whole, madly rushed Mini project was at risk. It was at this point that the man who saved the day came forward, a stolid but exceptionally ingenious Yorkshireman called Bill Cull, who was rumoured to be able to bend metal like a latter-day Uri Geller. He is a neglected hero of the Mini story.

## Chapter Three
# Bill Cull to the Rescue

*'I'll sign the cheques. You get on with getting the thing
to work.'*

Sir Leonard Lord to Alec Issigonis, July 1958

 BILL CULL WAS POOTLING ABOUT with some
metal screwthreads at the Rzeppa Works in
Shipley, on the edge of Bradford in the
industrial West Riding, when the call came
from Birmingham: 'Is that Unipower? Could
you kindly put me through to the managing director's
secretary?' The anecdote gives a misleading picture of a
business which was actually based in a small part of a former
tram garage by a suburban roundabout; Rzeppa House was
not a lot grander than the proverbial inventor's garden shed.
But what was going on inside it was truly impressive, and the
future of BMC's secret new baby car project depended on it.

For twenty-five years, Cull had been puzzling away at
what in today's terms might be called the Mother of All
Universal Joints, a beautiful piece of engineering called the
Rzeppa Continuous Velocity Joint whose complications are
fascinating even to someone such as myself, who scored the
lowest attainable grade in physics-with-chemistry O-level. I

was offered one at the 2009 Mini Fair for a tenner; even beneath a coating of grime and with a patina of oil streaks like beer stains on a pub carpet, it was beguiling. A sphere like the ball of a knee joint, it sported finely cut grooves full of ball-bearings, which could bend the direction of motive force through almost any angle or stress.

Cull had bought the rights to the best of a series of patents registered between 1926 and 1934 by an American of Czech origin, Alfred Rzeppa, who worked as an engineer at Ford's in Dearborn, Detroit. Some of his joints had been tried by the company and one version was used in the famous US Army Willys jeep. But they had limitations, and from the late 1930s onwards Cull worked away at painstaking improvements which he patented in turn. He noted how stresses forced Rzeppa's ball-bearings against the edge of the grooves which contained them, gradually wearing the metal down. The sequence of his drawings shows how he tackled this by experimenting with different shapes of groove, finally settling on one which looks in profile like a small Gothic arch.

Like Issigonis and Lawrie Bond, Cull was an outstanding product of his time and place, and as such an appropriate contributor to the Mini revolution. A Northern grammar-school boy, he grew up in a world of manufacturing where making things was both an honourable profession and fizzing with inventiveness. Like the neighbouring Calder Valley, which produced three scientific Nobel prizewinners in Cull's time, the small towns along the river Aire such as Shipley were prime breeding grounds for future inventors. William Cobbett wrote of its factories, men as well as masters: 'They have that quickness, that activity, that buoyancy of spirits, which bears them up through adverse circumstances.' Towering above Cull's lock-up were the two enormous mills built in the 1850s by Sir Titus Salt, who disproved the general assumption that alpaca wool was impossible to spin and made a fortune out of mohair. There were many more modest but similar concerns. Across the streets of Salt's model village of Saltaire, which is now one of the United Kingdom's twenty-eight World Heritage Sites, was the birthplace of the tumble-dryer. Its inventor, William Spooner, son of the Oxford professor responsible for spoonerisms such as 'the shoving leopard' and 'a well-boiled icicle', was a Shipley textile engineer whose brainwave came from watching lines of local washing tossing and tumbling in the wind.

Cull learned his trade in another of these enterprises, the Scott Motorcycle Company, which employed an elite corps of specialised engineers in Shipley led by its founder Alfred Scott. He pioneered the high-speed two-stroke engine and then set up the Scott Trials for motorbikes in the Yorkshire Dales to test his products against rivals. It would be prime-time sports TV today, but in the 1920s its spirit was caught more modestly in the annual programmes, which included poetry such as this skit on John Masefield's 'Sea Fever' by a regular competitor, Frank Duncan:

I must go up to the moors again, to the craggy moors and sky
And all I ask is a stout bike and the strength to steer her by
And the wheels' kick and the gears whine and the rear wheel biting
And the blue smoke with its sweet reek and the zest for fighting.

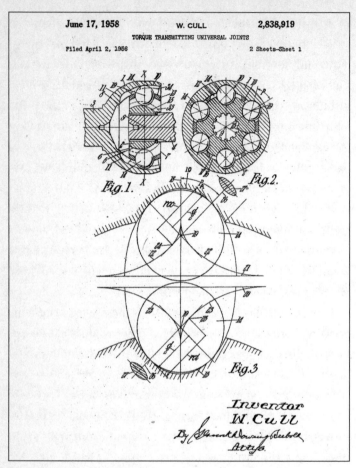

June 17, 1958    W. CULL    2,838,919

TORQUE TRANSMITTING UNIVERSAL JOINTS

Filed April 2, 1956    2 Sheets-Sheet 1

*Fig.1.*

*Fig.2.*

*Fig.3*

Inventor
W. Cull
By
Attys.

This was the spirit of Issigonis' love of hill-climbs and sprints in his Lightweight Special sports car, and the Scott set-up also had the practical cast of his way of working. Like him, its engineers experimented with all manner of vehicles to test the high-quality parts made by men such as Cull. Issigonis made a wartime mini-armoured car for one soldier called the Salamander, an amphibious jeeplet called the Gosling and a larger version called the Guppy which was later, appropriately, renamed the Mudlark. Scott's produced the Sociable, a cosy three-wheeler developed from a machine-gun carrier in the First World War, and the Squirrel, a hefty motorbike whose engine was adapted to power the almost suicidal self-build miniature 1930s plane, the Flying Flea. The firm's mechanical engineering was sound as well as clever, and the brightest of the team was Bill Cull. He designed the Flying Squirrel and, after Scott's death from pneumonia brought on by his unquenchable enthusiasm – he motorbiked home in wet clothes on a freezing day from a potholing trip in the Dales – Cull effectively took over and saved the company from bankruptcy.

Later he moved on to set up his own business, the grand-sounding Unipower of Rzeppa Works, whose principal market for his super-joint was submarine periscopes. The Cull-Rzeppas were too good for standard motor vehicles, an unnecessary luxury; he was working on this, but earning enough to continue patiently with his obscure work. The sudden light which shone on him from Birmingham came thanks to a BMC engineer at Cowley in Oxford who was even more widely read than Issigonis, and heard about his colleague's frustrations with the driveline of the secret Longbridge baby car.

He was Syd Enever, the chief engineer at MG in Abingdon near Oxford, and he shared Issigonis' habit of scouring the technical press for innovative ideas, not just motoring journals and papers but much more widely, including regular scrutiny of engineering brainwaves emerging from the Patent Office. He recalled an interesting joint which he had read about in an article on submarine periscopes, tracked it down, drew a sketch and scribbled an outline of the principles which he sent across to Longbridge. It was Cull's latest and best, and as soon as Issigonis absorbed its cunning hinge at the point where power transmission bends, he knew that he had got what he wanted. Very big wheels were set in motion.

The upshot was that Unipower was bought, lock, stock, barrel and, most importantly, Cull himself by Birfield (Birmingham-Sheffield) the parent company of the best-known manufacturers of universal joints in the world, Hardy Spicer. The whole operation was moved to Birmingham where Cull stepped up his work on further perfections to the joint and, equally important, designed the machine tools to make them, a skill he had also learned at Scott's in his Squirrel and Flying Flea days. Issigonis' hectic pace infected the whole project. A new factory was built within months and 40,000 Cull-Rzeppa joints were ready to supply to the new assembly lines at Longbridge and Cowley as the future Mini came onstream.

Cull is not a name you will find very often in the Mini's history. Issigonis did not like to share the credit, even with fellow-engineers who would never have suggested that their role in the car's creation was comparable to his. Even Hardy Spicer was initially a bit grudging; a junior colleague of Cull's, Peter Wheeler, remembers how a group of senior managers made difficulties about the great man keeping his company Riley Elf – a slightly souped-up brand of the Mini –

when he retired. Wheeler, who had greatly enjoyed curious discussions with Cull on such subjects as what the toggles of the Yorkshireman's duffle coat were made of, plucked up courage and challenged them. 'For goodness' sake,' he said. 'If it wasn't for this man, none of you would have jobs.'

They made up for it later. On the fortieth anniversary of the Mini in 1999, Hardy Spicer published a commemorative brochure to celebrate its part in the making of the world-famous car. There is the great Sir Alec's photograph, shaped in an oval like a medallion of Caesar garlanded with olive leaves; but beside it a second portrait gets equal billing, the same size and shape as Issigonis' and with the same satisfied air. It is of Bill Cull. Not only that, but the text below describes the Mini as 'a revolution in driveline engineering and passenger car design' – in that order. Jolly good about the miraculous creation of space, is the message, but just look at our Bill's wonderful joint.

Cull himself felt well rewarded. When he told a friend of his, Jack Poole, a metallurgist in Keighley who helped him with his metal 'bending', about the Hardy Spicer buyout, he added with a grin: 'If I can crack this, I'll be a millionaire.' The deal did indeed go some way towards that, and Cull lived comfortably into his mid-nineties. When Poole called to see him at the age of ninety-three, he was experimenting with the cooking times of different-sizes of cubes in a microwave oven and insisted on his friend making notes. 'When it came to the Mini,' Poole told the obituary writer of the Bradford *Telegraph & Argus*, 'Bill had the right thing at the right time, and he got it right.'

Things were better but still not right at the experimental workshop in Cowley, where Cull's joint relieved the secret team's biggest problem but left others unsolved. Before going on to his second and third revolutionary steps, which involved the gearbox and tyres and suspension, Issigonis had to sort out which power unit his new baby was to have. It was a real business, according to Bob Grice, who was Longbridge's Apprentice of the Year in 1959 and spent time attached to the Mini project. He was particularly well aware of its 'separateness' from everything else at the plant because his father, Geoffrey Grice, had the enviable title of Chief Experimental Engineer at Longbridge at the time. Grice senior shared in the widespread scepticism at the plant about what was going on in the 'Issigonis cell' as it was often termed, appropriately for a factory with an HQ nicknamed the Kremlin. For him, the new baby car was an experiment too far: a flyer, albeit with senior management support, which was best kept at one remove at the furthest end of BMC's South Works. His own days were taken up with amendments to the existing Longbridge fleet; he was noted for work he did on solving collapsing suspension on the Austin A40 and steering defects on the Riley Pathfinder which, Bob laconically observed, 'could have led to deaths'.

The family actually had three generations in the plant at the time, which was not atypical of the enormous workforce gradually assembled by Herbert Austin and maintained by successors after his death in 1941. Grandfather Robert Grice was a skilled carpenter who transferred after the virtual disappearance of wood in cars to work as an inspector of engine valves, father Geoffrey the high-flying engineer, and Bob the apprentice – and one bright enough to get shifts with the Issigonis team.

But he carried on talking, all these years later, not so much about genius as the problems which beset the future Mini. 'We were all given to understand that there was a remote possibility that there could be a breakthrough here, but that it wasn't likely,' he remembered. Even with the Cull Rzeppa joint on board, it looked less and less likely, as the team grafted initially at a specially designed new Austin engine. The work of Dr Joseph Erlich, it seemed outstanding on the factory testbed, but malfunctioned repeatedly once fitted in a trial car and taken round the twisting roads and steep inclines of the Lickey Hills. 'We spent hours on it, but couldn't work out what was wrong. It remains an interesting, unsolved engineering problem,' said Grice. Curious engineers can inspect the Ehrlich engine at the Motor Heritage Museum in Gaydon, where it finished up. It played no further part in the Mini story.

Instead, the workshop had a go with a two-cylinder engine, similar to the sort used in some bubble cars, but it was 'terribly rough', according to Bob, and simply lacked the guts. 'We needed a car which could do over 70mph, which was reckoned very fast in those days. The two-cylinder just didn't have it, not with any comfort anyway.' It was soon dismissed in favour of an apparently unexciting third choice, the Series A engine which was the reliable Austin workhorse of the time. Thanks to the unprecedentedly small size of the proposed new car, this brought the opposite problem to the two-cylinder: it was *too* powerful. On a test run behind the Lickeys, two of the team turned their test car over and came back shaken. In a sense, they had created a Mini Cooper before its time; but the charwomen thought to be waiting for the car were not in that league, and the unit was scaled down by 100cc.

Then there was trouble with the synchromesh gears, which struggled to cope with the Mini's stack of novelties: not just the transverse engine and its gearbox cleverly tucked underneath in the engine sump, but also the front-wheel drive and the little car's low clearance. All the experimental kit broke and a secret deal was done with Porsche, which made the best synchromesh system in the world. 'It seemed brilliant at first,' said Bob, who took out a trial car fitted with the new parts. 'But then it broke too.' There were days when the whole team tore its hair out as solutions seemed to come, but only lasted briefly before leaving the old questions unanswered as before.

It is fifty years ago now, but Bob recaptures both the frustration and élan of the group, as he recounts how the Porsche gears were finally adapted to work, and a completely baffling and thoroughly alarming glitch apparently affecting the Cull joints was traced amid sighs of relief to another component, part of the driveshaft. 'Like the Ehrlich engine mystery, it never happened on the testbed at the factory, but always did on the road,' he recalled. Then he reached over for my notebook and in his neat engineer's script wrote out three different equations involving horsepower, work done and stress/torque, one of them dating back to the days of James Watt.

Bob learned these skills in part through contact with the

Issigonis experts, who forged on with their other innovations as each problem was investigated, analysed and cracked. The car's second great innovation after the transverse engine was the hidden gearbox, placed inside the sump and using the engine's own oil to function smoothly. This saved further space and, like the engine-shift, proved Issigonis' brilliance at making real the ideas of others. Instead of protruding back towards the driver, the box was now tucked away and encased with the engine – another idea originally outlined, but not pursued in practice, in a specialist motoring article like Pomeroy's, this time in *Autocar* in 1952.

After that, cabin space was finally fixed by the creation of uniquely small ten-inch wheels, positioned right at each corner of the car, which gave Dunlop's specialists headaches before they could produce sufficiently robust tyres. The bubble cars reappeared at this stage in the process; Dunlop used a Gogomobil to test the strengthened rubber needed for ADO15's much greater speeds; and until these were ready, the first trial Minis were fitted with actual bubble-car tyres, which had never had such a battering before.

Dunlop's rubber skills involved them in the third engineering revolution in the Mini's works, a system of rubber cones instead of steel springs, which allowed independent suspension to go with the front-wheel drive. It was designed by Alex Moulton, who later became famous for his folding bicycle. Moulton was another of Britain's ingenious, car-minded engineers who inherited the inquiring mind of his father, John Coney Moulton, an entomologist who became director of the Raffles museum in Singapore and discovered a number of previously unknown butterflies and moths. Alex also specialised in searching for the unknown and doing the not-yet-done. He built his own steam engine when he was fourteen and went on to set up a combined, small-scale factory and inventing laboratory in the outbuildings of the Hall at Bradford-on-Avon, a magnificent Elizabethan mansion which he inherited and was understandably reluctant to leave.

He was also a little cautious of working too close to Issigonis, whose eagerness to drive the project on sometimes turned into peremptory treatment even of close colleagues. A stickler for correct procedure, the designer would sometimes hurry to the workshop where the more relaxed and affable Jack Daniels was sorting out problems, and pretend that he couldn't see him because he wasn't wearing the manager's standard white coat. Colleagues remember him raising his voice and asking peevishly: 'Jack! Where are you Jack?' and then instructing Daniels in front of the rest of their colleagues that the coat was always to be worn.

This worked with subordinates but less so with outsiders, such as the leader of a team of specialists from the electrical firm Lucas who were assigned to work with the project team on equipment for the Mini. Summoned to Longbridge to discuss the matter, he was asked by Issigonis what sort of dynamo he would recommend. Instead of proposing something as novel and exciting as the rest of the car, he suggested Lucas' existing and pretty standard C93 unit. 'Ludicrous! Far too large!' replied Issigonis, explaining with as much patience as he could muster that everything under the bonnet had to shrink to allow the Mini its seating space.

'You had better design a smaller unit — and have it in production in six months.'

Not used to being treated like this, the Lucas expert remained stubborn, until Issigonis drew in his breath and reached for one of the 100-sheet Arclight detail tracing pads which he used for his sketches and calculations. 'See this?' he said, handing over a swift pencil drawing of the coming car. 'That's what my car will look like.' Then he handed over another sketch, adding, 'And you want it to have an electrical power source like this ...' The second drawing was of Battersea Power Station. It was no joke so far as Issigonis was concerned, but he did not get a new dynamo. Lucas refused to budge on the C93 and privately they reckoned the Mini would not last in production for more than a couple of years. As the specialist recalled in retirement: 'It was such an oddball concept. There was no way our Board would sanction product development expenditure on a piddly little dynamo for what they often referred to as a piddly little car. In their view, it was doomed before it even went into production.'

There were many other more familiar parts in the Mini's mechanics, borrowed rather than created by Issigonis and his team. It was the way they were put together that was so different and radical and, once assembled, this cutting-edge work had to be tested particularly thoroughly. There was a high premium on secrecy; the workshop itself was isolated, and screened from Bristol Road trams by shrubs and a line of large trees. The emerging baby car was so unlike any predecessor that its shape was hard to disguise, but, at twilight on the works' internal roads, strange camouflaged shapes began to be seen as 1957 wore on. Some had the Austin A35's distinctive radiator fixed to the front, others were scratched and daubed with paint as if they were one-off specials from some lone enthusiast's workshop. Occasionally, they left the factory after dark and drove fast up into the Lickey Hills, one of Longbridge's favourite testing grounds for prototypes. A long incline is topped by a sharp left turn at the church where Lord Austin lies buried. As well as paying their respects, the test drivers, including Issigonis himself, could have a good run through acceleration, gears and brakes.

ADO15's name also began to change, in ways which added to outsiders' uncertainty about what was really going on in the experimental workshop. In the tradition of the Austin Cambridge, with an added bit of punning on its unknown future buyers, the car became the Austin Newmarket. Then, at the Paris Motor Show in 1957, Issigonis and his closest lieutenants were enjoying a coffee in Champs Elysées after dinner, when they noticed everyone in the street was looking up at the sky. They were hoping to glimpse the Soviet spacecraft Sputnik, the world's first orbiting satellite. 'It's going around the world. I wonder if our little car is going to go round the world,' mused John Sheppard, Issigonis' assistant designer and fellow engineer. After that, the first six of the car's twenty-four prototypes were nicknamed Sputnik by the team.

The project became even more furtive as the cars went further afield, using tricks of disguise from both Austin and Morris's long history of skullduggery over new models. Both Cowley and Longbridge had an unofficial network of obscure sideroads in the Cotswolds which were used at night by test cars. Issigonis liked to recall a strange meeting on one of them years earlier near midnight, between himself at the wheel of an experimental Morris Minor, and a rival car engineer, Ian Duncan, who was driving an under-wraps prototype called a Fedden 1Ex, which in the end was never built. The decent thing in such rare circumstances was to stop, get out and give the other car a very quick once-over without saying anything, then drive off. But Issigonis couldn't resist saying afterwards that he knew at once that the 1Ex was a no-hoper.

The decency of outsiders wasn't to be relied on, and the major tests of the Mini took place behind the wire and dense shrub screening on the perimeter of Chalgrove airfield between Oxford and Thame. To this day locals remember talk of the secret 'baby car' hurtling round the bumpy roads of the former wartime base, which remains wired off because the Burns Martin ejector-seat company still uses the site for its own tests. A few miles away at Garsington was a celebrated tree which Mini test drivers from Cowley circled at speed until the front joints started knocking. I spent a drowsy summer day looking for it and found an obvious candidate in Sadlers' Croft, on a tiny roundabout which now shelters an allotment and a carport. But local residents knew nothing about the tales of orbiting Minis which have become part of the car's legend. Doug Wheeler, who has run a repair garage in the village for forty years, shook his head and said, 'Sorry, doesn't ring a bell.' When I knocked on the door of the family who owned the carport, they told me: 'People round here object to the noise made by Garsington Opera. Whatever d'you imagine they'd say about cars racing round and round?' Perhaps the secrecy measures somehow concealed the manoeuvres; but we concluded that the tree must have been further down towards the factory, in fields developed for a 1970s housing estate.

There were near escapes from the car's details being revealed. Mr Druce, the science teacher at Colmer Farm secondary school in Longbridge, managed to get his sheaf of technical details to show his students. And the tightly knit Issigonis cell included an occasional adviser who needed to be watched because one of his other experiments blew off part of a workshop roof. He was John Morris, an expert problem-solver who sometimes pitched a children's wigwam in his living room when he needed to think undisturbed. No one was hurt and outsiders were successfully discouraged from asking too many questions about what had gone on.

Two of the closest shaves involved Issigonis himself, once when he was having a meal with his friend, and fellow cosmopolitan Englishman, Peter Ustinov. Naturally curious and lively minded, Ustinov chatted about car design and asked, a propos his friend's mysterious new project, 'Why does nobody think of putting the engine across the car?' Issigonis went pale, according to Ustinov's own account, but within months he was taking chances himself.

He had gone on a skiing holiday in the winter of 1958 with the family of George Dowson, one of his earliest collaborators in car design, and was acting as uncle to Dowson's son Christopher, a role at which he excelled. The two of them made a Meccano version of the secret Longbridge car which, according to young Dowson, was recognisable. They then ran it up and down their hotel's corridors and Issigonis even went to the lengths of sending chambermaids for supplies of olive oil to lubricate the toy's clockwork motor. Luckily none of them were agents for Volkswagen or Fiat.

By then, it was too late to change. Issigonis had passed the fateful challenge issued by Lord at the height of the Suez crisis, by creating a car which would make any bubble burst. He now took the chairman for a high-speed run in the most heavily tested of the prototypes, known from its lurid livery as the Orange Box. There are two different accounts, both stemming from Issigonis, of what Lord said as he unpacked himself from the tiny car. One is: 'Alec, this is it. I want it in production within twelve months.' The other is simply: 'Build it.' Lord's deputy George Harriman also came over from the Kremlin to the project's workshop to see the car and decided: 'It's very tiny, but it's good.' Both men were bowled over by the masterful engineering in such a small space, genius which dazzled away any doubts about the Mini's future.

One person did have doubts, and that was Issigonis himself. For all the supreme self-confidence which he displayed in public, he was by his own confession suffering sleepless nights, worrying about the enormous amount of money and the number of jobs riding on his ability to get the car right. He said afterwards: 'When Len Lord told me to go ahead and build it, I was horrified. I even told him he was mad to build a car on what we had been able to demonstrate at that stage.' As he dashed about the Longbridge works, he looked at the enormous complex of buildings and the daily tidal flow to work and back of his thousands of colleagues. Did their future lie in his hands?

## Chapter Four
## Trouble in Minitown

*'A pretty disastrous venture.'*
Sir Terence Beckett, former chairman of Ford UK,
describing the Mini in 2002

 WHERE HAS IT ALL GONE, NOW? Like the statue of Ozymandias in Shelley's poem, the mighty works which made the Mini is today a wreck. Piles of ground-up rubble lie behind security fences prowled by security men in pretend police cars. Hoardings optimistically announce: 'We are clearing the way for a brighter future', and developers' signs point the way to Egg Hill and its promise of 'vibrant urban communities' once the 2009 recession is through. In the middle of the mess is a small, just-beating pulse of industry, the modest operation of China's Nanjing Motor Corporation, which bought the bulk of the British Leyland marques and is making a handful of new MGs a week. If you ask nicely, they will show you the silent old works museum where star Minis and a range of unbuilt prototypes stand, dusted and buffed up regularly but seldom seen.

'So where was the secret workshop?' I asked Bob Grice, as we squinted through the big mesh fence on Lowhill Lane and studied a forlorn pile of pulverised bricks. 'Just there,' he replied, pointing at the nearest of several rectangles of rubble which had once been BMC buildings. 'The one beyond that empty beer bottle, left of the dandelions. That's where we worked on the Mini idea, well away from all the rest of the works. And I can tell you, I wasn't the only one who thought the Austin A35 was an extremely good car and couldn't see any need to replace it with this unknown thing.'

Bob is a polymath who changed tack after five years of Mini production, and retrained in 1963 to become a lawyer and then a lecturer in law. Driving along the back roads to Longbridge from his home in Redditch – another network of quiet lanes where early Minis were tested – he discusses in turn the difference between the words 'among' and 'amongst', the recent exhumation for possible sainthood of the remains of Cardinal Newman (from Rednal cemetery on the Lickey Hills test route) and Liberal Democrat politics, in which he has been involved for much of his life. He was specially pleased when we got on to Alex Moulton, and the role of his rubber suspension in the Mini's crammed package of new thinking. 'Moulton defied Hooke's Law!' he said excitedly, reliving the moment in 1959 when it became clear that the new rubber cones got round the venerable eighteenth-century scientist's rule that a spring extends in direct proportion to the load applied to it. I was momentarily late in lighting up my face in response. 'You *do* know Hooke's Law?' he checked. I fudged.

The team at the far end of the Works didn't fudge, ever. Grice has a lot of the philosopher in him but he remains an engineer. One of his daughters got involved in his long-standing anxiety about 'among' and eventually sent him the *Guardian Style Guide* produced in 2008 by my colleague David Marsh. 'It was such a relief to find a yes-or-no approach,' Bob said. 'Marsh doesn't mess about – he just says, "Use among."' The instruction had the same precision and pithiness for Grice as Robert Hooke's actual sentence: 'As the extension, so the force.'

It was this kind of certainty which the Mini team was seeking, and bit by bit they applied it to all the challenges thrown up by Issigonis' challenging notepad designs. 'He was quite a genius in thinking it all through and drawing it out, but it brought *so* many problems,' said Bob, in a heart-felt tone which showed how easy it still is for him to relive them. He and the others often gave up free time at week-ends, wrestling with the apparently endless challenges, and sometimes he wondered if the whole enterprise was too little grounded in the real world.

'We had a department headed by an academic, a Dr Wearing, who had a PhD and was probably in the vanguard of university-type research, but wasn't at all practical. People used to say that nothing useful ever came out of the place, just intriguing ideas. I regarded Issigonis as more realistic than Dr Wearing, but there were times ...'

There was also a difference. The Issigonis cell genuinely worked as a team, even if 'Aragonis' could behave as though everything depended on him. They were hand-picked and enjoyed the resulting *esprit de corps*, the sense of being an elite. They were diverse too. Issigonis tried to enlist Doreen Schreier, who had broken the Cowley engineering department's male monopoly and came to work on the first Morris Minor to have its headlights raised from the original low level to meet American safety standards. He was upset when the problems of finding housing in Birmingham were too tricky for her and she opted to stay at Oxford.

More modest craftsmen were vital to Issigonis too. Cull's joints were part of a complex operation which depended in turn on very skilled and diligent BMC staff who could fit them, and all the other components, into the highly engineered car. They are still easy to find in retirement, many in the streets surrounding the old factory site. A particularly good hunting-ground is Herbert Austin's model community, the Austin Village, which has just celebrated its centenary in fine style. A short walk down Longbridge Lane from the railway station and past some tower blocks, you enter a different, self-contained world. Narrow, leafy avenues are lined with clapboard bungalows like an American suburb, their gardens smothered with clematis and climbing roses in June. These are the survivors of 500 homes ordered in one huge lot from the Aladdin company of Bay City, Michigan, in 1917. Part of the consignment was sent twice; twelve railcars packed with red cedar timber and 48,000 lbs of assorted nails were lost when the *SS Headley*, carrying them across the Atlantic, was torpedoed by a German submarine. But Herbert Austin had an enormous influx of extra war workers to house and he simply had the consignment despatched again.

In the village lives Doug Adams, who has only strayed a couple of streets from the Aladdin house where he was born, the year his father moved from Burton upon Trent to take charge of the Austin company's stores at Longbridge. Brought up surrounded by woodwork, he told his father at the age of fourteen that he intended to be a joiner, but was quickly put right. 'You're not going into that,' said Adams senior firmly, anticipating the future which saw Bob Grice's grandfather move from joinery into engine inspection. 'It won't be long before there's no wood any more in any cars.' Looking back today, when metal has reigned for years apart from ornamental dashboards, Doug agrees: 'How right he was.'

The young lad clearly had design sense, however, and it was this which brought him into direct contact with Issigonis during the Mini years. After an apprenticeship in panel-beating, and following the death of his father aged thirty-nine and his mother shortly afterwards, he was to some extent 'looked after' by the sympathetic firm. Thus he came to have regular contact with the new car's experimental team. As Issigonis developed his ideas, men such as Adams played an important part in the detail, although they learned to adjust their approach to the great man's way of working. 'You had to, let's say, *suggest* there was a problem,' the retired engineer explained with a gentle grin as he remembered his early dealings over the Mini. 'It was fatal to say, or even imply, that you were right and he was wrong.'

At one of his first encounters, Doug also sensed the need to hold his tongue. 'I was summoned to the Kremlin and he' – Issigonis is always 'he', the only, dominating 'he' in most junior colleagues' recollections – 'was there with Battista Pininfarina. They'd been discussing the chrome strip at the front of the Mini and he says to me: "I want it that much smaller. Can you organise that?"' Issigonis demonstrated the cut he wanted made by pressing the end of one of his thumbs against the other, leaving a gap in the nail which Adams had to reckon on the spot.

'You mean three-eighths?' he asked cautiously. 'No,' said Issigonis, 'I mean that.' And he repeated the gesture exactly as he had before. Adams had to take a mental snapshot and trust his own judgement. It almost certainly was three-eighths, he reckons now, and certainly Issigonis didn't quarrel with the resulting trim. But it was the way that he, and therefore they, had to work.

Experience turned Adams into a skilled adaptor of Issigonis' sometimes problematic ideas, for example a speedometer whose installation would have been complex for the men who had to fit it on the assembly lines. Handed the component by Issigonis, Adams went no further than murmuring in his soft Brummie voice: 'I'm not sure what the production people are going to think about this.' Issigonis gave him a quick look but said nothing. Two days later, he was back with an adapted and much less fiddly version plus an instruction to Adams to 'get our production people down to have a look' before the part was finally approved. 'He was in charge and brimming with ideas,' said Adams. 'But my colleagues and I were the ones who had to get the things *made*.'

The ones who had to make them *fit* are also still easy to

find, past the stretch of the Bristol Road through Longbridge where an overhead bridge once took half-finished Minis to the paintshop on automatic tracks. Between this and the railway line into central Birmingham lie the low-slung buildings of the Austin Sports and Social Club, where an older but still vibrant ex-factory community is only too ready to remember the Mini days, and how tricky things were.

'Oh, it was a terrible car to put together,' Ray Diprose recalled over his pint. 'They all said you could tell the Mini line, because everyone working on it was old and grey-headed from stress. It was nothing like a modern car, where everything's packaged and fits exactly. Nothing lined up. You had to make it fit. Every car was slightly different and there were problems like paint drip. Imagine, you had a threaded part which fitted into a bolt, and it gets a bit of paint on and jams. Oh, it was a terrible car to sort out.'

Ray worked in 'Body and Whites', where the 'white' or unpainted panels – bonnet, roof, doors and the rest – were welded together before the cars were painted and then taken back on the assembly line to have everything else put in. One of the commonest problems was that the body shell was dropped on to the frame from the separate overhead track which moved at a different speed from the main, floor line carrying the rest of the car along. The crunch came when the open-top cabriolet model of the car was introduced, with extra engine parts. 'I told them, "There's no way that's going to fit", and it didn't,' said Ray's friend Trevor Dodsworth, who joined the Number Two spraying and rubbing down shop at Longbridge in 1963, five years after the launch of the Mini and when it had taken off as a fashionable car. 'The first cabriolet ended up on the assembly line with its top part tilted half on and half off. They had to rethink the process, and add the extra parts after the bodyshell had been fixed on.'

Swiping in members from his booth by the front entrance, the club doorman Colin Manders is another Mini-making veteran, a multi-skilled 'slip' worker who stood in for members of one of the eight-strong bodywork assembly crews as they took their morning and afternoon breaks. They were in the old West Works, now another clearance site, and their job was to fix the doors, fenders and bonnets on Minis as the cars travelled along the assembly line. The process went at a snail's pace but it was still demanding for the fixers to get the job done within the length of their allotted section. 'See up to those doors,' said Colin, pointing along a brightly carpeted corridor between the club's wood-panelled walls. 'That's about fifteen yards, and that's the length we'd have to get the job done. If we didn't, the assembly line would stop, and the gaffers didn't want that.'

A slipman like him stood in for each member of the crew in turn, going off to get his own break when they had all had theirs. For half an hour, Colin would be a door fitter, then for another half-hour he would be doing fenders. The bit he didn't like was the bonnet, which involved walking backwards in a space in the middle of the assembly line, working away at the hinges as the car moved slowly forward. 'You used airguns for the bolts and it was all quite complicated,' he explained. 'But the trickiest thing was gauging the exact fit of the parts.' Panels brought over by truck from Fisher Ludlow in Castle Bromwich weren't always quite right, and it was the bodyparts crew who had to sort that out.

The Longbridge works was enormous, employing 21,000 people at its peacetime peak in 1960 – in the two world wars, extra munitions work took the total on site to 32,000, one of the largest concentrations of working people on the planet. It grew out of determination of one man, Herbert Austin, first and only Baron Austin of Longbridge, who took over an old printing works run by a company called White & Pike by the river Rea in 1905, when he was thirty-four. At the plant's zenith, between 1960 and 1971, when it turned out a record 318,475 Minis, it took three-quarters of an hour to walk from the eastern boundary to the tip of the West Works. Engines were trucked in at the rate of 15,000 a week. Even when closure came in 2005, the 6,500 remaining staff were the tip of a pyramid of suppliers who employed another 27,000 people.

Like his creation, Austin was a big man, decorating his office with a picture of a powerful-looking steam engine above the motto: 'Most everything worthwhile is born of some Dreamer's dream.' Dismantled when the previous HQ was demolished and moved en bloc, the room has been preserved inside the ghostly museum now owned by Nanjing, hidden away in the factory's last reception building. Still embedded in the original wood panelling is the half-crown which Austin tossed in 1921 to decide whether or not he would close the plant after the cancellation of wartime government contracts. On one of the other walls is the present the workforce gave him after the coin-toss went in favour of reprieve: a barometer, symbol of how conditions, economic as well as meterological, can change.

Colin's section of the factory prepared a sort of skeleton of the Mini, the whole of its outer bodywork, which was then grabbed by a hoist, trundled over the Bristol Road bridge, and sent through the paintshop to the engine and chassis workshops. Plenty of completed shells headed off elsewhere, on a branch track just before the hoist to the 'boneyard', a temporary resting place for car parts with flaws. 'There had to be four or five people by the hoist,' he said, 'checking in case something had been missed out or not fixed quite right.'

The whole process could be nerve-wracking. When he was 'bonneting', Colin had two tracks moving close to his legs on either side, grinding along with the cars also attached to another track moving slowly overhead. If upper and lower got out of synch, it played extra havoc with the fitting work; even worse was running out of the parts to fit. 'You couldn't go anywhere. Your job was to stay in the section and do the fitting. You just had to hope that the guys responsible for bringing the bonnets or doors or whatever got to you in time.' He remembers people pressing the emergency button to halt the line in desperation, and also nasty accidents when it failed to stop in time.

Standing in as a slipman, like the similar 'sick and relief' jobs which backed up the regular crew, meant extra training, but not very much. 'I had a month and a half in the training school rather than a week,' said Colin, who started in 1976 when there were six Mini lines going full pelt. As demand dropped, they were cut to two and the bodyshop was 'demanned', with Colin and his mates transferring to the Austin Allegro.

He is good at explaining what he did, thanks to practice with celebrity visitors. One afternoon, he got a tap on the shoulder, turned round and there was Prince Charles. 'You had to concentrate on the job so I'd not noticed him coming, even though he had about twenty bodyguards and quite an entourage. He says: "Hello. What do you do?" And I told him, "I put the bonnets on."' A couple of years later there was another shoulder tap, and this time it was Noel Edmonds. 'He was making a commercial for Rover, but he just wanted to know where he could get some aspirins. He had a splitting headache.'

Colin was long out of car-making by the time we met, but he liked the history which is still tangible in the sports and social club. He knew the plaque commemorating its opening by Austin Rover's then chief executive H.J. Musgrave off by heart, and points out where the formidable apprentices' boxing team had their ring. Now it's a conference suite and car park, with no old Minis in it but a couple of the bulgy new BMW ones. 'My first two cars were Minis, proper ones,' he said. 'They were cheap and nippy and ever so spacious and they got you from A to B.'

Back in the bar, where the one-day cricket international down the road at Edgbaston was flickering away on Sky Sports, more former Mini workers were thinking back to the old days. Trevor and Ray were recalling muddles in the supposed sequence of cars as they entered the paint shop. 'They came along the line in all their different types – saloon, Cooper, traveller or van,' he remembered. 'At least, they were supposed to, but of course it often wasn't like that.' One of the hassles was having to find a new spray gun or rapidly clean and refill the one you were using, if a car unexpectedly jumped the colour sequence.

'Automatics were a real pain as well, weren't they?' chipped in Ray. 'They had that many extra parts, which all had to be sprayed. There were a lot of things like that which caused extra work and didn't seem to be planned for.' Another one was the fetching of different parts for each Mini from plants as far away as South Wales. 'The Government wanted to share the work out all over the country, which you can understand,' said Ray. 'But it complicated the process of putting the Minis together.'

The hassles soured relations between management and men, and Longbridge was notorious for disputes and walkouts. 'We all hated the actual work,' Trevor told me bluntly. 'You were there to make money, get the job done and then go home.' He and his colleagues are still convinced that a lot of the trouble was deliberately provoked. 'If they needed to cut production, they caused problems for you so that you'd walk out,' he explained. 'We came back from holiday once to find that all our tools had been boxed up and dumped in the Ponderosa' – another boneyard, where parts waiting for use lay outside and often came back to the line rusty or even, in Ray's experience, needing snow brushed off them. 'We complained about it and they said, "Well, you go and fetch them." "Hang on," we said. "You put them there, so *you* go and fetch them," and back and forth it'd go until we walked out and they got the reduced production they wanted, because they hadn't sold so many cars over the holidays.'

In spite of the men's cynicism they did try to take up shoddy work with managers, at least in the Mini's early days. There may have been dodgy 'Friday cars', made on the last shift before the weekend when everyone wanted to get away, but the crews didn't like seeing a sub-standard car leave the factory under the radar of quality control. 'We'd say, "People are paying £500 for these cars, we shouldn't be giving them a duff one,"' said Trevor. 'But the answer was always, "Don't worry, they can get repairs done under guarantee." It was like galvanising, which might have stopped the Mini from being such a rust box. I heard a professor from Birmingham University saying it would only have cost ten shillings a car, but they wouldn't have it.' If someone's Mini dissolved in rust, they might buy a new one.

The result of all this was the us-and-them dogfight which made Britain's car industry notorious in the 1970s and early '80s. The shops were 100 per cent unionised and the works was known as the 'Madhouse', alongside the 'Kremlin' that was the management block, although there was nothing Communist about those inside. That was left to the likes of 'Red Robbo', the most famous of Longbridge's union activists. Colin, Ray and Trevor all knew him, and there were nods from others at the table when Trevor said: 'I didn't necessarily agree with his politics but I'll tell you one thing: he was as honest as the day is long. I'd sooner trust him than any of those we had in charge at the works.'

Both men left in 1998, two years before the last Mini came off the Longbridge line. 'I could see the way it was going,' Ray said. 'I don't know how it lasted so long.' He ticked off the inefficiencies which lamed the car as a profitmaker, including a huge variety of different carpets available on order. The men knew that each Mini was reputed to lose money, which reinforced the 'madhouse' school of thought. 'The managers had a little blue book which wrecked everything. It was their Bible, all the production targets they had got to reach, and they were just obsessed with that.' Quality seemed to come second, to the embarrassment of the firm's most senior staff, including the chairman Leonard Lord. He bought the promotional number-plate BMC 1 but soon disposed of it, according to his daughter Pauline, because angry customers kept trying to flag him down to complain about problems with their cars.

The Mini's compensating fame as a symbol of Swinging Britain largely passed the factory by, although Ray remembers some enthusiasts, such as a rep from a firm called Monroe who supplied the car's shock absorbers and was another of the tall men somehow attracted to the car. 'He had seven or eight Minis, one after the other,' he recalled. 'And he was a great big man, six foot four inches at least. He had four of them in his family, and they all piled into the Mini to go on holiday every year. He loved them.' Assembly-line workers seldom saw the high-ups either, although a cousin of Trevor's met Alec Issigonis when he was a boy. 'His granddad worked on the early Minis and helped develop the indicators, and Issigonis went round to their house a couple of times.' Whatever the result, it didn't make life any easier for the assembly teams.

Mini-making wasn't all bad, though. The men may have been there for the money, but the money was good. Trevor moved to the plant from Cadbury's, which is two stops down the railway line at Bournville, because of the wage rates. 'I was thirty-six with two kids and I had a job for life at Cadbury's. But they were paying £14 a week (£219 today), and I went straight on to £29 (£437) here.' The stress of fitting together Issigonis' revolutionary car was much heavier than making Dairy Milk and Brazil nut chocolate, but the rewards were more than twice as much.

There was also camaraderie among the assembly-line workers. Trevor and Ray remembered Sailor Bill, one of their section's regular crew, who always came in on Monday mornings far too drunk to be trusted with a rivet gun or paintspray. 'We'd hide him at the back of the shop to sleep it off, and come dinner time he'd be back in action,' Ray laughed. 'After that, he'd always cover for anyone else who wanted a bit of a break. That was the deal.'

Pranks were part of life. One of the paintshop team was a keen gardener and brought in Brussels sprout plants for a colleague. While they were out on a break, the rest of the crew unwrapped the plants, cut off their roots and then carefully packaged them up again. 'The next morning,' said Ray, 'the air was blue.' More subtly, another would-be gardener was given a packet of seeds by an older colleague with the promise that they would fill the patch in front of his house with colour. They were all beetroot plants. There were fishing clubs, darts leagues, table-tennis ladders and football on the unforgiving hardcore outside the workshops. 'There was blood all over the place,' said Ray with a grin.

The sentiment still brings them back to the club, and to regular reunions where they pal up again with the likes of Rolls Royce Jimmy, who started at Longbridge at fourteen and worked on the first Minis in 1959, and the sheet-metal workers' shop steward, Burglar Bill. He got the nickname after taking his tools home during one walkout and getting stopped by the police late in the evening at Halesowen. Sorting through his bags of jemmy-like implements, they took a lot of convincing that he wasn't going house-breaking. Ray still has his book at home of all the part numbers for a Mini. 'I know them by heart,' he said. 'I can't remember my Army number, but I'll never forget them.'

Given these complexities, and the demanding deadline imposed on the project by Leonard Lord, it is not surprising that the new car went into production with problems unsolved and glitches waiting to happen. Some were caught in time, including the discovery that the way the transverse engine had been placed exposed the carburettor, at the front, and led to a risk of it icing up. That was solved by lifting out the engine and turning it 180 degrees, still transverse but with the carburettor now snugly at the rear. Much worse was the leaking of water into the car through poorly designed floor joints, a feature of the early Minis which had customers making pointed remarks about the need for wellies and umbrellas on wet days. Victims included BMC's own publicity operation at the 1959 Motor Show, whose brochures were reduced to a soggy mess after a rainy drive on the M1, and a test team in France, who used bricks to keep the passengers' feet clear of water slopping round the floor. In desperation, they drilled more holes in the bottom to drain the lake as rapidly as it was filled through the gap in the floor panels. Another tester filled his Mini with a hosepipe and then lay on the road noting exactly where the water was coming out.

Issigonis was circumspect about the water problem in later years, claiming that the fault had not come to light because the car had been given its final tests in the heatwave summer of 1959. But he made his own list of fifty-one other defects, including mysterious rattles, clutch and synchromesh difficulties. Such teething troubles were to be expected in new models, but this was quite a tally. The biggest error, however, was nothing to do with Issigonis or anyone else on the design team. It was the fact that when the car was launched on the market, it was seriously under-priced.

Bob Grice told me that at regular intervals during the ADO15 project, he had suggested solving problems with more expensive components. The reply had come back down the chain of command: that would be fine if we had the budget of the Riley Pathfinder, but we're not building a Pathfinder. Although Leonard Lord had put all the resources of Longbridge at Issigonis' disposal, the Mini was meant to be a cheap car to own and run, in keeping with the belief that its role was to triumph in an era of expensive petrol and drive the bubbles into oblivion.

In practice, and in spite of the brush-offs for Grice's suggestions, the engineering in the new car was so radical and unlike anything else on the road that the bill was proportionately very high. It continued to be so, because of the assembly difficulties described by Colin, Trevor and Roy. If the effect was to turn their hair grey, it was also to turn BMC's balance sheets red. The car's retail price had been worked out by methods which no one in the car industry with accountancy training could understand. The basic model in 1959 was priced at £350 (£6,096 today), as close as dammit to the mechanically far inferior Ford Popular which Lord and Harriman appeared to have taken as their benchmark rival. The Popular was discontinued that year, and its successor the Anglia 105E, which took on the Mini on Ford's behalf, cost £380 (£6,618), a full £30 more. Ford went to the lengths of buying a Mini to dismantle and cost, and came to the famous conclusion that each car lost its makers £30. They wrote to Lord's people twice, in the clubbish way that business rivals often do if a product or price level seems to be maverick. But BMC was delighted to have undercut Ford, which had traditionally produced Britain's cheapest car. Financial planners at Longbridge were confident that the price would attract mass sales and that volume would bring profit. They were wrong. The man behind Ford's new models, Terence Beckett, later chair of both Ford Britain and the Confederation of British Industry, said bluntly: 'You can trace the decline of BMC from that single product. It took up a huge amount of resources, it sterilised cash flow and it was a pretty disastrous venture.'

Disastrous? The wonderful Mini! Yes, that was the word used by Beckett, who was to car pricing and marketing at the time what Issigonis was to design. We shall see why at more length shortly, but now, in the rosy glow of the launch and in spite of the bargain price, something else went wrong. The wonderful new car received a rapturous welcome from the motoring press, and a warm welcome generally for its tiny size but roomy space and gutsy performance. But did people queue to buy it? They did not. For its first year, the Mini languished well down the table of new car sales, to the extent that Longbridge contemplated closing down one of its assembly lines. Drivers didn't seem to want Issigonis' amazing creation; an attitude which seems completely unthinkable when you go to one of the many gatherings of Mini enthusiasts which take place today. Let's do that. Come with me to Mini Fair 2009.

## Chapter Five
# A Stuttering Star

'On looking at the door bottoms, I found two rubber plugs
which I at once extracted, and out flowed large volumes of
water. I would advise all owners to look at their own cars
and do the same thing.'

Letter to Autocar magazine from new Mini owner
G. Davies, November 1959

IT WAS A DULL JANUARY DAY but the queue to
the county showground wound back to the
edge of Stafford. There were very few Minis
in it, just the red and white top of a Cooper
ten cars ahead, but when we reached the gates
it was a different matter. Neatly parked on either side were
hundreds of the familiar, neat shapes, pairs of them huddling
together like courting couples and others in long rows with
common symbols showing that they had come as a gang.
Ten new MINIs, which are now allowed to join the annual
British Mini Fair provided they go in a corral of their own,
bore chequered flags snapping from those plastic window
clips which are everywhere during football World Cups.

As we parked in the field opposite the main entrance, a
Citroën people-carrier pulled up alongside and a family

tumbled out, Dad, Mum, two boys in specs and a younger girl. My first Mini fans. I made the usual cars-are-a-man-thing assumption and headed for the Dad, who introduced himself as Warren Harris, a haulage contractor from Whittlesea near Peterborough. But he promptly diverted me to his twin sons, John and Jacob. 'They're the ones who've got us here,' he explained. 'They're stripping down a Mini they bought two years back, on eBay.' Jacob and John were only ten then, which is young to start restoring a car of any kind. But if they were small, so is the Mini and that was part of the appeal. 'Their uncle had one and they liked the size of it and the design,' Warren continued, as the two boys waited shyly for a word. 'They're practical, and they had their Grandad's haulage yard as somewhere to learn to drive a car.'

Warren seemed content to have been taken at his word by his sons, who are identical twins and have identical views when it comes to Minis, and identical determination. They badgered him about getting one of the cars and, not sure how serious they were, he offered to pay for it if they could find one for sale under £500. They went off and won an eBay auction when bidding for a 1983 Mini Mayfair stopped at £435. 'It was taxed and tested and it looked all right,' said Warren. 'The seller seemed a decent bloke. He said the only thing was, there was a bit of an issue with the brakes.'

Jacob and John grinned their identical grins at this classic bit of car enthusiasts' language. But the brakes don't matter any more, because the boys are patiently stripping them, along with everything else, cleaning and repairing each part and ready to scout around at Mini Fair for replacements and experts' tips. While I was chatting to Warren and his wife Emma, and Penny was discovering their daughter's own Mini plans ('I'd like one as well, but only if it's pink'), they flicked through the photo files on their mobile phones. 'Here's the car,' said John, angling his mobile away from the light, to show a neat little Mayfair, painted black like my own son Tom's. 'We've probably got a couple more years' work on it, but it'll definitely be ready before we take the driving test.' Meanwhile, Warren has used one of his firm's diggers to cut a track for testing and driving practice on a patch of waste ground.

We'd been chatting on the way into the showground, a tunnel under the A518 between Stafford and Derby, and now we were back in the daylight and surrounded by Minis, drawn up like an army, albeit a very unmilitary one with the hundreds of smiling radiator grilles and headlamp eyes. The Harrises had to get on with looking for advice and spare parts, and as we said goodbye, Penny and I spotted something which had to be checked out. A Mini with a kitchen sink.

'Actually it's a doggie's drinking bowl,' said Ian Ottley, a helicopter engineer from Somerset, who had a kettle simmering on the gas hob which was also part of B933 YCC's equipment. He had drilled a hole through the bottom of the bowl and found an appropriately sized plug on a chain, using skills which at work he applies to Lynx helicopters bound for Afghanistan. 'Every Mini should have a bit of helicopter in it somewhere,' he added, showing us more of his handiwork: just a few of 200 changes he had made to the wiring alone. Like the Lynxes, his car isn't going to suffer any unexpected electrical faults.

Ian's collaborator in the adaption, Richard Leigh, came up and introduced himself, a professional metal 'prepper' in the motor trade, a man who strips and straightens, cuts and fills. He has his own Mini, silver and with a gas barbecue attached to the back, but his efforts have recently been concentrated on Ian's. 'It's actually three Minis,' he explained, starting with the main bit which left the factory as a basic 1000cc Mini City. 'By the time I bought her in 2002, she had a 1380cc engine. We joined her on to a trailer [the bit with the kettle and sink] and the back end of that is a bog-standard 1988 City.' The more glamorous front of the whole contraption was cut off a 1985 Mini Sprite.

The car attracts endless attention and that, apart from the engineering fun, is the point for Ian and Richard. They are always going on charity rallies, helping most recently to raise £36,000 for a children's hospice on the Grand Tour of North Devon in 2008. Later in the year comes the International Mini Meet at Longbridge, another fund-raiser, and yet another attempt to break the record of working Minis driving in convoy. The third member of the team, Philip Hayes from Halesowen, was meanwhile chatting to the owner of the next Mini in line, an adaption called Stunt Dad painted in the blue and white livery of Cadbury's chocolate bars, which had sponsored the car. 'He's got a detachable front to get at Issy's tiny engine,' he reported back, and there were nods of approval all round.

The approach to the main hall was lined with a double file

of beautifully restored Minis, all for sale at tempting prices: £4,595 for a 1997 Mini Mayfair in metallic peacock blue; £5,795 for another from the same year, but with twin exhausts and a lot of extra stuff beneath the raised bonnets. Other bonnets were opening and then shutting with that familiar, gentle clunk. 'Aaah,' sighed the woman keeping an eye on the more expensive of the two Mayfairs. 'They're so light, you hardly get a bruise if you drop them on your hand.' Inside the building, Mini mania was in full force, with the Carroll family from Featherstone busy wrapping up a roll of window trim filler and negotiating over a secondhand hinge panel. 'You know how the door starts sagging in an old Mini?' asked Geoff Carroll, an engineer who was temporarily out of work and so concentrating on restoring a Mini in his garage. 'This thing holds them up again.' His wife Karen interrupted: 'Actually, Geoff usually makes his own from templates, but we thought it would be good to have a proper one too.' Cutting out the templates is the job of the Carrolls' daughters Hattie and Rachael, who were managing to play with their identical yellow Slinkies between stalls, as well as carrying the roll of window trim. 'They snip them out of cereal packets,' said Karen. The Carrolls are ingenious altogether; Geoff has made a giant version of a barbecue spit which rotates the Mini when he needs to work on its chassis or roof.

Both girls are Mini fans too, but the car's followers come a lot younger than that. Next to Newton Commercials, where the Carrolls were buying their bits and bobs, was a stall selling Mini babygros for three-month-olds and tiny T-shirts bearing the car's smiling face. The crowd pushed on past a woman demonstrating how easy it was to clean leather and vinyl Mini trim. 'You can walk up and down on it after stamping in the showground mud,' she said, doing just that, 'and it will wipe completely clean afterwards.' She got out her J-cloth, and it did. She introduced herself as Maggie Lawton, purveyor of trim in hundreds of colours, running a company near Blackpool which was founded by a passionate Mini man who previously lectured on classic car design at the University of Central Lancashire. Then up came another customer, whose eighteen-year-old daughter was doing up a Mini entirely in pink, Emma Harris' dream car. Maggie listened and then said decisively: 'Candy Pink, nice and bright. That's the colour for you.'

Colour co-ordination wasn't the thing upstairs in the show hall's galleries, where several dozen Minis had been driven via the ramps which normally take the prize animals of Staffordshire farmers. In a rainbow of 1960s hippy colours, the staff of Hilltop Minis of Malvern had created a painstaking stand designed as a tribute to the car's great Age of Cool. 'I used sixteen yards of floral paisley to make this,' said Jan Judge, who runs the business with her husband Richard. 'I got it on eBay for £3.' Both were swathed in authentic flower-power wear: enormous coats, long billowing skirt for her and massive flares with floral panels for him, red bandanas round her long blonde hair and his gently balding head. 'That's the one thing that's not quite authentic,' he admitted, indicating what looked like a dead animal hanging down the side of one of several deckchairs which, along with heaps of other stuff, were props to show how much the Mini could hold, a recreation of a BMC advert in 1959. 'It's my hippy wig. It was getting a bit tickly.'

Jan and Richard's Mini was even more eye-catching, one of six runners they own plus another which is currently out of action in a chicken shed. They had painted the one for the Mini Fair in authentic psychedelic swirls, much to the delight of the girl on the till at the Morrisons filling station in Malvern, who told them: 'I was conceived in one of those.' (Actually, for all the stories told by lustful owners, the standard Mini has never been good for that sort of thing.) When they go for a drive in their oldest and most distinguished Mini, a Mark 1, they always get questions like 'Has it got sliding windows?' or 'Does it use one of those floor starter buttons?' followed by 'Oooohs' of satisfaction when the answer to both is Yes. Another of their collection, a 1978 T-reg, is named after their sleepy old golden Labrador Charlie, because both have loud, popping exhausts.

Jan went into the motor trade after starting early, like Paula Cooper in the Bubble Car Museum. She ground valves at the age of four for her father, a mechanical engineer at ICI in Birmingham, who was doing up an elderly Morris Oxford in his spare time. 'You get caught up in it,' she said, watching approvingly as a procession of fellow enthusiasts pottered past, one absent-mindedly clutching a complete radiator grille, another looking like the Tin Man from *The Wizard of Oz*, he had accumulated so many spare metal parts.

Hippy they may have been, but Jan and Richard had one lapse from authenticity: they were much better-scrubbed than I remember being in my flower-power days. Not so Bruce Mills and his exhibit a few stalls further on. He still had mud on his boots and trousers and his 1978 GT Mini, registration AGY 926T, was covered in the stuff. This was the opposite end of fandom to the beautifully tricked-out Mayfairs in front of the hall entrance, or the care which had gone into the swirls and loops of the Judges' psychedelic car. Mills, a mechanic from Kidderminster, specialises in hurling Mini racers round dirt tracks in the Midlands, up against monsters such as Voodoo Ford Escorts or a TNT Tyres Mitsubishi which doesn't take any prisoners.

'That's genuine mud from Ludlow,' he said, scraping off a wodge of the brown stuff mixed with little stones from the Shropshire town's annual gravel sprint. 'I've fitted her with a cheap bonnet 'cos you quite often hit things on these rough drives. There's no petrol cap either or anything else sticking out. Trouble with that sort of thing is, they tend to get stuck in trees.'

The last port of call for Penny and myself was at a pair of record-holders, the oldest Mini at the fair and, next to it, comfortably perched on a camping stool and taking occasional swigs from a bottle of ginger beer, a man with long hair in a Panama hat who owned more Minis, by a stretch, than anyone else we had met. 'I've about twenty, I think,' he said, introducing himself as David Troth, a retired engineer, whose garden on the edge of Bromsgrove over-flows with the little round shapes, as does the adjacent garage. 'The family's had the house since 1908, so I feel I can make the cars at home,' he said. They include both an

Austin Se7en and a Morris Mini-Minor from 1959, a Mini-Moke, two pickups and a K72 Cooper S. But the one he has chosen to bring to Stafford to show off is a Minivan – 'A purchase-taxi, we used to call them,' he said, 'because you didn't pay purchase tax so long as you bought it with only a seat for the driver.' This was the world of Christine Perry and her boyfriend back in Longbridge in the Mini's earliest days; but although cheap and convenient it had one or two bothersome requirements. David pointed out a small parking light which had to be clipped to the battery if you parked overnight on a main road, a legal requirement in 1960. The van, a beautifully maintained model built that year and registered VDL 619, had only one previous owner, a woman on the Isle of Wight. Demand for excellent old Minis is such that when David bid for it at auction, he set himself a limit of £10,000.

He didn't have to pay that much in the end. But it is the sort of price which might be fetched by the lovely Mark 1 Mini standing next to his van, a Tartan Red saloon, UMU 777, which was only the 483rd Mini to be built, completed at Longbridge on 16 July 1959, a month before the car's official launch. It had soft grey and red leather upholstery and a set of special extras for its buyer, the Rev. Hubert Victor Nicholl-Griffiths who was vicar of Zeals, near Salisbury. Among them were four picnic baskets, fitted below the back seats and in the side-pockets made available by the car's sliding windows. Like the clever little space in the Messerschmidt bubble car, these freed up the space lower down the door which in rival cars was taken up by the window-handle mechanism. Rev. Nicholl-Griffiths presumably had something milder in mind than Issigonis' gin bottles for parish outings in Wiltshire.

The vicar of Zeals was a contented customer, and after a day at the Mini Fair, it was hard to think of the car doing anything other than sweeping all before it. Penny and I were completely Mini-ed, even tempted to put in an offer for UMU 777 because 16 July is Penny's birthday. Hard to imagine, then, how different things were as 1959 turned into 1960. The now famous car was struggling to attract buyers on the large scale needed to justify BMC's investment. Production in 1959 reached only 19,749 and sceptical sales staff at the company, who had privately warned that the design was too radical for the largely conservative British car buyer, began to worry that their fears had been justified. Winter brought water penetration to light, first in problems with damp distributors and that dismal clunk when the starter motor turns but nothing else happens. Then came the increasingly dramatic descriptions of flooding from the floor. More and more cars were recalled to the factory or dealers for adjustment, a process which can banjax a new model's prospects as word spreads that it is 'difficult' or prone to repeated faults which the makers seem unable to iron out.

Concern spread to the press, which initially had given the car an unstinting welcome. On display on the back seat of Rev. Nicholl-Griffiths' Mini at Stafford was a copy of the *Daily Sketch* published on the day of the launch, 25 August 1959, with the lead headline 'Some Baby', above an article which started: 'The most sensational popular car ever put on the roads will be uncovered in the showrooms this morning.' That was quite something; how many new cars today would get the front-page splash? Think of the extraordinary advances in engineering made, for example, by the hybrid electric-and-petrol cars such as the Toyota Prius. They had to be content with news stories well into the papers, or features on the motoring pages.

The general, non-specialist public at the time of the launch was therefore well aware that something technically excellent had happened and that it was proudly British, for all the peculiar name of the man who was given most of the credit. 'Issy wissy what's his name?' Lord Nuffield had crudely lampooned him, and inevitably there was a bit of that from the man and woman in the 1959 street. Even BMC's commentator in the official launch films calls him 'Issigoni' without the final 's'. But without understanding the precise technical details of what he had done, people were happy to hail the breakthroughs and to nudge one another as the strange-looking car was revealed on TV and say – as Christine Perry remembers her neighbours in Longbridge reacting – 'Just look at that. Now isn't that something different?'

The specialist press was naturally seriously excited by the technical wizardry beneath the bonnet, with *Autocar* at a loss to find any previous car which 'contained so much that is entirely new'. *The Motor* considered the roominess in particular 'miraculous' and the whole package 'a remarkable combination of speed with economy'. Its reviewer added: 'Characteristics which have often been thought utterly incompatible are combined amazingly well.' Other technical writers reacted like scientists looking for the first time through an electron microscope at some insect or mollusc organism. How could something so small contain such complexities? Why had engines and transmissions been so big for so long?

But the little box of joy began to look more like Pandora's version as the days went by. The launch was lamed from the start by BMC's fusty tradition of maintaining the divide between the various famous marques which it had absorbed. The theory was that continuing the rival names of Austin and Morris as if they still had a separate existence would make customers feel that any new car inherited those glorious mantles. The reality was that a single brand became a muddle. Although I have referred thus far to the new car as the Mini, to avoid confusion and because that is how we all know it today, the most important thing to realise about its launch is that it *wasn't* the Mini then. Half the cars were called Austin Se7en 850s, from Longbridge, and the others Morris Mini-Minors, from Cowley. There was no substantial difference between them, apart from radiator shape and the bonnet badge. And soon both were being made at each factory.

The confusion worsened when more, although admittedly slightly more varied, versions appeared as the Riley Elf – and the Wolseley Hornet. And every aspect of the cars' production and marketing was split in the same way too. There were thus two launches of the thrilling new car, at Longbridge and Cowley, and extraordinarily, two versions of the main twenty-eight-minute promotional film, which meant that sequences had to be doubled up everywhere from Norway to southern Spain. *The Incredible Seven* by Austin showed two Se7ens scooting about; *Wizardry on Wheels* two Mini-Minors, while the same Belgian petrol attendants gawped and the same clipped commentator observed that the drivers of VW Beetles overtaken on the autobahn were 'surprised out of their lives'. At the same time as this duplication, the different traditions of Austin and Morris kept trying to insist that there was some sort of difference, eventually lamely settling on the notion of twins, although without specifying whether they were identical. So was this one car or two? It was one, but that was not the clear, simple message which should have gone across.

Longbridge was historically less fleet of foot than Cowley, but its presentation of the new car was excellent. Curtains swept aside in a darkened room to reveal an enormous magician's hat. As spotlights flicked on, this parted to reveal an Austin Se7en from which, in a fine piece of amateur choreography by the sales department, a junior executive's wife and their five-month-old baby emerged, followed by three of the largest men they knew, a woman friend, two dogs, and boxes and bags of every size. Cowley followed with a similar piece of theatre but much better press releases. While the Austin marketing people (also kept separate by BMC's fatal internal divide) produced leaden material about the foresight 'of Sir Leonard Lord and Mr G.M. Harriman', their counterparts at Morris commissioned the popular *Punch* cartoonist Russell Brockbank and cheekily mixed endorsements with quotations from Leonardo da Vinci, Samuel Johnson and Lord Nelson.

Enough emerged from this porridge to make it clear that the new car was extraordinarily roomy and a doddle to park in busy towns. This was reinforced by more cheerful advertising films. 'The world is growing smaller; the world is growing more crowded,' one announced, showing a happy family on an outing with tennis rackets whose faces sour as packed London buses roar heedlessly past their stop. The answer? 'The nippy, zippy raring-for-a-trippy, gracious, spacious, incredibly capacious, willing, thrilling, rarely-need-a-filling' miracle car. But more evils from Pandora's box lay in wait. One was the belated realisation of how wrong Lord had been when he switched Issigonis from designing a middle-range successor to the Austin Cambridge and launched him on the 'baby car' in the belief that small cars with modest fuel consumption would be the transport of the future. By August 1959, Suez had long gone and petrol prices had fallen sharply and seemed settled. Prosperity had also resumed its onward march. The dominant social philosophy was keeping up with the Joneses. In these circumstances, did people with £497 to spend (£8,656 today), the basic car's £350 plus a whopping £147 purchase tax, want to use it to buy a 'charwoman's car'? They did not.

The Mini was bound to sell in reasonable numbers, come what may. Far too much investment had gone into the car to risk it becoming a total flop; it was BMC's leading new model, the first for nearly a decade, and the rate of production was set above that of the Austin A35 and Morris

Minor. In November 1959 Lord also announced an expansion plan for BMC costing nearly £50 million. But this meant that real success had to be on a comparable scale, and that was not happening. The fact that the target buyers were looking an extraordinary bargain in the face did not help. On the contrary, the underpricing of the new car was a self-inflicted wound for BMC and its successors in the long term, but it also made no sense as a marketing ploy at the time of the launch, so far as the middle classes were concerned. The Mini was actually cheaper than Isetta's bubble car. What do you think the Joneses would say about that?

The very Mrs Moppery of the Mini's radical design compounded these disadvantages further. On the Mini fiftieth-anniversary wall at the Motor Heritage Museum in Gaydon is a card signed simply 'Jill' about HEC 542, which her family bought early in 1960 and drove home to Westmoreland, where it was the first Mini ever seen. 'We got many strange glances,' she recalls, 'but the biggest challenge was coping with my eighteen-stone grandfather.' He wanted a spin in the curious little car and was shoe-horned in for a drive. Moulton's suspension sagged but the Mini took it. The only problem, Jill remembers, was: 'We had difficulty getting him out.' The car's astonishing size was miraculous, but not really wanted by many customers; and in the longer run it was to scupper the Mini's chances of global sales on the level of the VW Beetle. When federal safety standards were tightened in the United States in the late 1960s, the Mini failed automatically because it was simply too small.

The first models, including the so-called De Luxe version, were also stripped down to an almost military functionalism. Issigonis was famously insistent that a car was a means of getting from A to B as efficiently as possible, and nothing else. This was partly the result of his own personal austerity. He took his watch back to be repaired even when it was twenty years old, and designed and made his own lawn mower and other household gadgets. But he also disliked anything which might distract the motorist from concentrating on driving. In the 1970s, he was asked his opinion of the much more comfortable and well-equipped cars by then on offer to the mass market. He replied that they were 'much too sophisticated for my liking because I still enjoy driving without being surrounded by an environment of domestic and household appliances'. He never had any time for extras such as radios, and even seatbelts and other safety measures struck him as deterrents to competent driving because they risked inducing complacency. Why did the Mini not have reclining seats, he was asked. 'Why should it?' he replied. 'You don't drive lying down.' The idea of a car as a status symbol appalled him. He was especially mocking about drivers who bought a car because they liked the curve of its bumper or the colour of the upholstery, or some other such 'irrelevance'.

The Mini went the other way with a vengeance. Seams were welded from the outside because that was simpler and easier for the Body and Whites crews. What did it matter, in terms of driving, that the joints were therefore visible? Door hinges were fixed to the outside of the door panels and so were equally obvious. The door-opener was a length of plastic-coated wire which, like the starting button on the floor, dated back nearly thirty years to the original Austin Seven, which had replaced its floor starter as long ago as 1932. The instrument panel was just one dial with a speedometer and fuel gauge, plus two switches below for the wipers and lights. A heater had to be ordered as an extra. Even the De Luxe model did not have heating as standard, just some extra chrome trim on the outside, a bit of carpet and an ashtray.

This wasn't how you impressed the neighbours. Events were to prove in due course that Issigonis had actually designed a stylistic masterpiece, but there was only a suggestion of that in 1959. Almost alone, BMC's perceptive Italian style consultant Battista Pininfarina said on first seeing the car: 'Keep it absolutely the same, it is unique.' His celebrated countryman Aurelio Lampredi, of Ferrari, was more typical of the general reaction when he spoke admiringly of the car's technical brilliance – but added, 'If it wasn't so dammed ugly, I would shoot myself.' The long faces of BMC's sales people were matched by those of the car dealers, who had to shift the cars and had long experience of the public's taste and conservatism.

Lawrence Pomeroy understood why, even if Issigonis didn't. Now the editor of *The Motor*, which gave the car an extremely enthusiastic road test, he contacted his friend and put it to him straight. However much he might dislike it, 'there were buyers who rated the apparent attractiveness of the car outside their garden gate as considerably more important than ease of parking in cities, economy of running on highways, and cornering power on by-roads'. Using the conventional social categories of classbound Fifties Britain, he said that class D, the workers, 'regard the car coldly', but that did not matter too much because they were unlikely to buy a new car, or in many cases a car at all. The real problem was that B and C, the middle and lower-middle classes, saw the Mini as 'admirable but not buyable', since they would be smirked at by the Joneses for having a car which 'by being sub-size was by inference sub-standard'. For those who knew about the extraordinary technology, the Mini might be underpriced, said Pomeroy. But it seemed to be a poor deal for those who wanted something which looked impressive, or at least up to date.

For almost all these buyers, the Mini's other potential role as a second car, a woman's runabout in town, was not yet an option. Households with two cars were a rarity in 1959, when most of the country still had difficulty in affording one. The case for making the Mini less austere was unanswerable but initially Issigonis met it with a weary sigh. 'Yes, my dear Pom,' he replied, 'I know there are tens of thousands of such people, *but I will not design cars for them.*' It was inevitable that the mechanically conventional but more impressive-looking Anglia, which was launched a few weeks later by Ford, overtook Mini sales at once.

This was not a purely British phenomenon; the export market was equally sluggish, and for similar reasons. When the German car magazine *Motor Revue* reviewed the Austin Se7en in 1960 they concluded sorrowfully that although the 'miracle car' was much the most interesting of the ones they had tested, it fell down on simplicity and cost. 'Here customers often buy cars less perfect for more money,' the article concluded, 'but, alas, purchasers in our country lack clear vision.' The prevailing tone was like that which surrounded the demise of Concorde in 2003: a beautiful engineering masterpiece at odds with what the public wanted and could afford.

Perfect was also a dubious word at this stage. To add to its image problems, the new car seemed to have more than the usual share of teething troubles, especially the leaks. Soaked and smelly carpets joined the Mini-welly jokes and although the problem was solved within the first year, it was expensive for BMC because the car's floor had to be redesigned. Water also made the floor starter button unreliable, while oil leaks sprayed the clutch plate and the synchromesh often crunched. Hundreds of cars went back to Longbridge and Cowley for repairs.

All new models have teething troubles, but the Mini's were made worse by the sour atmosphere in BMC's factories at the time. Whatever their faults, the paternalistic founders of Morris and Austin, Viscount Nuffield and Lord Austin, had been regular and often surprisingly accessible figures on the factory floor. Nuffield did not forget that he had once been a mechanic turning out bicycles in a small Oxford shop. Austin was a Yorkshire farm bailiff's son who had worked on an Australian shopfloor making sheep shears. Lord and Harriman had many talents, but they could not match the aura of the two founders and they failed to make up for that with chumminess or the common touch. Working practices were Byzantine, as men struggled to defend piecework rates in the face of automation, but management was clumsy, and vulnerable to wider criticism of poor strategy and complacency about foreign competition. The workforces at Longbridge and Cowley were learning more about the wider world, in common with post-war Britons generally, and were increasingly aware of their rights. A general election was due in the Mini's launch year of 1959 and the Labour Party under Hugh Gaitskell was widely, albeit wrongly, tipped to win. Anything could start a row which would then escalate rapidly, and throughout the year the plants were plagued by both wildcat walkouts and official strikes. The worst came on 15 July when BMC sacked the senior shop steward at Cowley, Frank Horsman, and the next day, just as the Vicar of Zeals' Mini left the assembly line at Longbridge, the whole of the Oxford factory came out on strike. The superstitious may note that the walkout lasted until 13 August, thirteen days before the Mini's launch. Like Trevor Dodsworth, admitting to 'hating the work' and doing it for the money, few of the men making the car were working in a contented and eager frame of mind.

As business dragged, Issigonis held firm to his minimalist, functionalist views. 'You've got to be uncomfortable to stay awake,' was one of his uncompromising defences. Even less apologetically, he suggested that suburban housewives with money were stupid and bought Fords, apart from some intelligent ones who bought Minis. But BMC's marketing department could not be so lofty, and it cast around for ways of giving the new car a lift. The most effective was suggested by Pomeroy: that motoring journalists should be given special delivery if they ordered a Mini for themselves. George Harriman thought this over and took the scheme a step further: the journalists could take a car on loan for a year and then buy it if they wished at a pre-arranged price, or give it back to the firm. Eighty Minis were sent out on this basis, all with the Oxford registration letters GFC. Sceptics at the factory translated this as Gifts For Correspondents, but the cars soon proved significant. Their new drivers had influence and contacts. They lent them to celebs. They talked to friends about the new little car's extraordinary road-holding, nippy turn of speed and, most basically, small size, so convenient for bobbing out from their Fleet Street offices to see contacts elsewhere in London. The Mini was the handiest of metropolitan accessories; and in an unexpected and small, but hugely publicised, part of its market, that is what it now became.

## Chapter Six
## Saved by the Swells

*The reception was bad. Then to our horror, we discovered
that rich and intelligent people bought it first.*
*Alec Issigonis, quoted by Christy Campbell in*
Thoroughbred and Classic Cars, *September 1979*

THE MINI WAS SAVED FROM obscurity and the
fate of a might-have-been at worst, or
the Comet and Concorde at best, by one
of the unexpected marketing twists of the
twentieth century. There was a decorous rush
to buy it by customers who were never remotely in BMC's
sales plan. The most enthusiastic early owners could not
have been less like the cost-conscious devotees of small,
fuel-efficient cars whose supposed existence persuaded Sir
Leonard Lord to tell Alec Issigonis to go forth and destroy
the bubble cars. As for Issigonis' dream of a charwoman's
car: he was shortly to find himself out for a drive not with
any Mrs Mopp, but with Her Majesty the Queen.

Within two months of the launch, in October 1959, the
royal household took delivery of a blue Mini and made no
objection to a little publicity for the fact that the Queen and
Issigonis had taken it for a spin in Windsor Great Park. That

might have been the end of that, because, although the palace later added an unusual Mini Beach Car to its garage fleet, the Queen was seldom seen publicly in anything other than a Rolls Royce or, at Balmoral, a Land Rover. But her sister was.

Princess Margaret was the populist royal of the day, a precursor of Princess Diana in that people liked the way she enjoyed herself unstuffily, and most of them sympathised with her unhappy past. She had been forced to abandon her hopes of marrying a former RAF officer, Group Captain Peter Townsend, by Establishment pressure, because he was not only a so-called 'commoner', but divorced. By 1959, she had taken up with another non-royal in the personable form of Antony Armstrong-Jones, a talented young photographer and what used to be known as a man about town. He was acceptable to those with clout at Court, because he had no 'past' (at least not that they knew about) and although officially a 'commoner', he was at least the son of the Countess of Rosse. In due course the couple were married and Armstrong-Jones ennobled as the Earl of Snowdon to meet protocol's demands.

Snowdon was no society fop, however. He was lively and curious and from an inventive family. His uncle was Oliver Messel, the theatrical set and costume designer, and the *Punch* cartoonist Linley Sambourne was one of his great-grandfathers. He had his own sense of drive, developed from an unhappy childhood following his parents' early separation; when he spent six months in hospital with polio as a boy, his only visitor was his sister. He took up photography as a career, not an affluent gentleman of leisure's hobby, and his study of architecture at Cambridge

University led to his co-designing the aviary at London Zoo which carries his name. When he looked for friends, it was not only among the youthful fringe of high society in which Princess Margaret moved. He also sought out practical movers and shakers, especially engineers.

Among these was Jeremy Fry, one of the heirs to the Somerset chocolate dynasty, whose social connections also went with an inventive mind. I remember him from my days as a cub reporter on the *Bath Evening Chronicle* in the 1970s, when he lived in Widcombe Manor, a delectable mansion on the edge of the most beautiful city in England, which was known with good reason as the 'Golden House'. He was celebrity material, with the same racy edge as Princess Margaret and Snowdon. They led lives of a nature which only much later became acceptable among people generally. Fry had been convicted for importuning guardsmen for sex in London, and he brought up as his own daughter a child actually fathered by Snowdon shortly before the royal marriage. But Fry was also a serious engineer, a man enormously knowledgeable about pumps in particular, whose company Rotork was one of the symbols of Bath's revival from genteel decay during the years that I worked there. He also designed and manufactured a four-wheel-drive wheelchair and a high-speed mini-car ferry called the Sea Truck, and, perhaps most significantly, encouraged and mentored a bright young employee at Rotork called James Dyson.

Fry had known Issigonis since the late 1940s, when they met at sprint and hill-climbing races, driving rival lightweight cars which each had designed. Friendship developed from this shared enthusiasm and the pair went skiing in Switzerland regularly, Issigonis always wearing three-piece tweed suits and skiing badly but with great relish. On one of these holidays in the mid-Fifties, Fry invited Antony Armstrong-Jones along and he too clicked with Issigonis straightaway. He was driving a Morris Minor at the time and, on later holidays, if he wanted Issigonis to go out and join him and Princess Margaret in Davos, he would send a telegram which became a code between the two men: 'Windscreen wipers broken, come out at once!' Pomeroy was part of the circle too, and slipped a sly reference to Fry into *The Mini Story*: describing how regular clearing-out of the car's roomy door pockets was essential, he listed among typical drivers' finds penny bars of Fry's Chocolate Cream.

These illustrious contacts were of crucial importance when the Mini was launched and then appeared to falter so far as a mass market was concerned. Issigonis was invited to the royal wedding at Westminster Abbey in May 1960, sitting between Noël Coward and a former landlady of Snowdon from his young photographer days, and as a wedding present he gave the couple a Mini from Cowley. In no time, Snowdon and Princess Margaret were photographed nipping from palace to club in the little car, and thus began an extraordinary trend. The Queen's modest outing at Windsor might have been nothing more than royal approval of outstanding British engineering, a sort of precursor to the Queen's Awards for Industry. The Snowdons' appreciation of the car was different. Here was the highest of high society using the odd new car every day, and getting youthful fun out of it. They exulted in its roominess and carried out some of the first of innumerable attempts to set a record for the number of people you could cram in. They rang one another up and said: 'God, you won't believe how easy this thing is to park.'

Snowdon also did the Mini a particular extra service by understanding, exploiting, and therefore publicising, its gutsy potential. Foreshadowing the Mini Cooper, and with the encouragement of Fry, he sent his wedding present car back to Cowley with a request to Issigonis to rebore the engine and 'make it faster than anyone else's'. He engaged in an entertaining duel over the sliding windows too. The Snowdon Mini reappeared once again in the workshops with a request for conversion to wind-up handles. Getting wind of this, Issigonis countermanded it. Snowdon persisted, and in the end the designer compromised. The passenger window only could be changed, he agreed, although he was still worried about the effect on Princess Margaret's styled hair, and whether wind-ups would dispel her cigarette smoke as efficiently as the sliders did.

Snowdon owned three Minis in these early days, and the royal couple's example was quickly copied. In *The Mini Story*, Lawrence Pomeroy astutely quotes the witty art historian Bernard Berenson on this characteristically English phenomenon: 'They keep away from anything new until some person they know well and can trust embarks on it. Then when they see that lightning hasn't struck him, they all rush after him.' Issigonis was regularly seen having lunch in London with the couple and went on holiday with them. It was soon the case,

Pomeroy added, that company directors, at whom the car had not been aimed, had more Minis in their reserved spaces in front of a factory than the rest of the workers, who should have been interested in the 'charwoman's car' but were not, yet. His book, published in 1964, played its own part in accelerating the Berenson effect still further.

It was not the company directors whose conversion did most to popularise the car, however, even though their approval helped in terms of keeping up with the Joneses. More significant were the fashionable friends of Snowdon and his princess, and especially those who were pursued round the clock by the media. Among early Mini owners were Peter Sellers, King Hussein of Jordan and Christine Keeler, the model and prostitute at the centre of the Profumo affair, a saga of vice, Soviet spies and a compromised minister which was more significant in terms of Establishment mockery than as any real threat to Britain. Minis nipped in and out of the goings-on, paradoxically to their great benefit: this was the little car at the centre of big things. Not only did Keeler have one but so did the other two main dramatis personae. John Profumo, the compromised Minister of War, possessed an appropriately lurid, scarlet example; Mandy Rice-Davies, another of the models-cum-prostitutes who frolicked at Cliveden mansion, both owned a Mini and had been hired at the age of sixteen by BMC to drape herself over the new Austin Se7en Countryman at the 1960s Earls Court motor show as Miss Austin. The car, in 1960s terminology, was where it was at. In today's argot, it was cool and – increasingly said as a compliment by people who couldn't care less about the Joneses, except the Armstrong- ones – it was cheap.

The rush to buy, which began in 1960 and accelerated over the next five years, was accompanied by another new way of looking at the Mini. Far from a status symbol, it was classless, as Snowdon himself proclaimed: 'I don't belong to a class. I never have. I had a Mini because it was fast, economical and great fun. We had different engines and the one we put in at the end was incredibly fast – a lot faster than my Aston Martin.' This was going it a bit, for the son of a countess who went to school at Eton, but it was appearance which mattered rather than reality. Snowdon's set made a point of publicly disavowing their inherited privileges and mixing with bright young things from very different backgrounds, the likes of the actor Terence Stamp, the photographer David Bailey and the model Twiggy, a super-mini herself. He was right to say that classlessness was the impression the Mini gave.

If Snowdon was the man who saved the Mini, the woman who gave him sterling support was Mary Quant, another of his set; the famous images of her boyish face framed by black hair cut in a distinctively angular, short style, are by Bailey. Quant was a latter-day Coco Chanel, one of the brightest of a postwar elite of students at Goldsmiths College in London who struck out in a completely new direction in women's style. The child of London teachers, she had a ragamuffin upbringing as an evacuee on the Kent coast, collecting souvenirs from crashed planes with a gang of friends until she was sent to boarding school at Tunbridge Wells. This and a youthful business she started with her brother in the holidays, teaching rich kids to sail, brought her into contact with the posh. There were more of them at Goldsmiths, where she met her future husband Alexander Plunket Greene. The combination of free thinking and good contacts was ideal for when she launched her ground-breaking clothes at Bazaar, a cramped outlet below Plunket Greene's restaurant in the King's Road, and Britain's first boutique. With her Mini parked outside, all black livery and black leather seats, plus a tin of Caran d'Ache crayons and a bottle of wine in Issigonis' wide door pockets, she launched dozens of other innovations: the Booby Trap bra, patterned stockings, detachable white collars, skinny-rib jumpers, the mod look and, of course, the miniskirt. The two great mini icons went together naturally, she said, 'because neither is any longer than absolutely necessary'. Swinging London was built on both; the visiting American essayist Tom Wolfe wrote admiringly of Mini cars and girls in miniskirts parading up and down the King's Road.

This was Quant's doing. She considered her practical but zippy Mini to represent 'true emancipation' for a woman, and she encouraged her models and customers to buy one too. Indeed it became all but essential for them to have one, if they wanted success: every famous, beautiful, Quant-styled young face was a Mini owner, from Jean Shrimpton to Paula Noble, who resprayed her Cooper twice a year to match the changing colours of her clothes. Quant echoed Snowdon's celebration of a new classlessness; it was limited in retrospect but dramatic at the time, after years of social inertia when the young tamely did 'the right thing'. As she said in 1966, when Bazaar had expanded vastly, with Quant designs in 150 shops in Britain and 320 internationally: 'There was a time when clothes were a sure sign of a woman's social position and income group. Not now. Snobbery has gone out of fashion, and in our shops you will find duchesses jostling with typists to buy the same dress.'

And the same car. In a reflective lecture on 'Urban Experience and the Automobile' in 2004, Iain Borden, Professor of Architecture and Urban Culture at the Bartlett school of University College, London, spotted another key face of the Sixties; lively and attractive rather than model-beautiful, but a princess among trend-setters and a customer of Quant. 'Look at this publicity shot of an English television presenter,' he said, clicking on to his next Powerpoint slide, and up came Cathy McGowan of the TV show *Ready, Steady, Go!*, smiling in the driving seat of *her* new Mini, while another part of Swinging London is under construction, with scaffolding and cranes, in the background. 'An image clearly intended to make a strong connection between McGowan, the city, the car and the act of driving,' argued Borden. 'Here is a symbol of female independence and cultural innovation. In particular, it is not just the ownership but the driving of cars like the Mini which helped to create this kind of everyday democracy: driving, that is, as a kind of exuberance, of playful darting around city streets.' Spot on.

Barbara Hulanicki of Biba had one too, and like Quant encouraged their use. The Rev Marcus Morris, a vicar who had gone into publishing and proved brilliant at it, launched a new magazine in 1962 called *Small Car and Mini Owner* which went unerringly for celebrities. Famous to my generation for the backward-sloping 'M's with which he signed his editorials in the respectable home's comics, *Eagle*, *Girl*, *Swift* and *Robin*, he was later to get the contract for the British *Cosmopolitan*. Penny, my wife, who was chief sub-editor of *Cosmo* in the 1970s, once sat on his knee in a car full of National Magazines executives. There must have been a lot of them, because it was not a Mini but Morris's company Rolls Royce.

There was a slight sense here of posh people slumming it, or playing at cars, but the enthusiasm was also practical. The primitive fittings were funky but straightforward, and if the Mini was a fun accessory it was also a sensible one. Here was a practical little car for negotiating London's traffic jams and needing minimum space when you had to leave it somewhere, to go clubbing or record a single in Soho or Abbey Road. John Cooper, who was shortly to play his own part in making the car more popular still, noted correctly: 'It was a toy car for them [the celebrities] really, and easy to park.' A posh person in a Ford would be using their chauffeur's car or an office one, he said, but if they were in a Mini, it would be their own. Peter Sellers agreed: 'For thousands of us who had to get round London quickly, the arrival of the Mini was like the answer to a prayer.'

In that entirely practical sense, the prayer had been answered at exactly the right time. Congestion in London was hardly new; as long ago as 1846 *The Times* deplored the fact that 'all our principal thoroughfares in London have become too small for the enormous stream of traffic poured through them'. But the rise in private motoring during the 1950s brought frustrations to a head; those objects of drivers' abuse the parking meter and the traffic warden made their British debut in Grosvenor Square in 1958 (when a Mr Nugent from the transport ministry ceremoniously slotted in the first shilling). In a Commons debate in December 1959 the transport minister Ernie Marples told MPs how his manicurist had complained to him only the other day that she could no longer park all day in 'her place' on a side road off Piccadilly. Happy times. The then Anthony Wedgwood Benn put the average speed of cars in London at 8¼mph and the annual cost of traffic congestion at £500 million. Privately, Marples wrote later to one of his senior civil servants explaining that he had bought a Mini because of the congestion: 'As Minister of Transport I must set an example.'

To dodge through this and then find a parking niche were cardinal virtues for the smart set in London; Princess Grace, Shirley Bassey and Margot Fonteyn bought Minis, as did Roy Boulting, who commissioned one with green and black vertical stripes and bought another for his wife, the actress Hayley Mills. Lord Hartwell, the owner of the *Daily Telegraph*, couldn't resist the trend, although his was chauffeur-driven. And like all the others, he helped the car's progress in another important way. They all referred to their new cars as 'Minis', rather than the official but cumbersome Austin Se7en and Morris Mini-Minor, and BMC eventually responded to what was clearly the public will. In January 1962, the Austin version was officially renamed the Austin Mini and in

September 1967, when the model's Mark 2 was introduced, the Morris car finally dropped the word Minor. It was a slow process but an unusual distinction for a car to be renamed by public demand – or at least public usage, because only the most pedantic owners ever stuck with the original versions.

Wider social trends were also beginning to work in the Mini's favour. In March 1963, the Beeching Report on the future of Britain's railways was announced on the BBC Home Service, followed by a funereal tribute to the 'stations with the beautiful names – Adlestrop, Midsomer Norton, Ashton-under-Wychwood' – which were among 2000 due to disappear. Their removal along with 5000 miles of line gave an extra spur to an already rapid increase in private motoring, especially in small cars. Traffic on Britain's roads had shrunk between 1938 and 1950 but nearly trebled by 1960, and it more than doubled again in the next ten years.

Mini production took off. In 1960 it overtook the Morris Minor by a clear 23,000 sales to become BMC's most popular car. The total of 116,677 rose steadily and in 1962 topped 500,000. By 1969 they had reached two million and the most productive year in the car's half-century came two years later, when 318,475 were made. The prolonged growth was helped by the equally sturdy staying power of the 'Swinging Sixties'. Famous buyers of the car are often strung together in a roll-call of the decade's celebrities, as if they all bought the car at the same time. In fact, seven years separated Lord Snowdon's British racing green Mini of 1960 and Steve McQueen's Mini Cooper S, fitted with a convertible roof and painted gold. The Beatles' famous cars were bought over a series of years: John Lennon's in 1964 (although there were widespread rumours of his using a chauffeur-driven one earlier, with smoked windows); George Harrison's Cooper S in 1965, originally black but later painted psychedelic as his music drifted that way; Paul McCartney's the same year, with Aston Martin rear lamps and metallic green livery; and Ringo Starr's in 1966, with extra room for his drumkit engineered into the design. Then the Stones took over, with Marianne Faithfull arriving by Mini at the Law Courts in 1967, to support her then boyfriend Mick Jagger over a drugs rap.

A look at any of these celebrity Minis reveals that something strange had happened to Issigonis' original simple principles. There was nothing remotely austere about any of the Beatles' cars, and Faithfull's had interior fittings worthy of a Rolls Royce. The funky plaything became a battle-ground for rival attempts to fill a small space as lavishly as possible with exactly the 'fashion items' Issigonis had decried. The outside of the car, originally available in any colour so long as it was red, white or blue, turned into a gadget-carrying rainbow. There was something about the boxy little plainness of Isigonis design which challenged ambitious and wealthy young owners. Paint me! Embroider me! Tart me up!

Peter Sellers was one of the first to strike out, fitting his series of Minis with painted wickerwork panels which made them look like large picnic baskets. The livery specialists Hooper's won the commission for Sellers' 1963 car, promising to give the job to one of their best craftsmen,

Geoffrey Francis. His talents were described at the time in *The Motor* magazine's report on the car as the work of 'the heraldic artist who has practised on Royal coaches and other distinguished conveyances for many years'. Lawrence Harvey went for a similar traditional approach, with his initials in gold on the doors of his £3,500 car, a price seven times higher that of the standard but mechanically almost identical model of the time. George Harrison had a cobra coiled under his petrol cap. The most celebrated 'art Mini' lasted only three days: a car hired by the *Sunday Times* in 1965 to use as the 24 October cover picture for a feature on the Swinging Sixties in their colour magazine – itself a famous product of the decade. It had been launched only three years earlier with the cartoonist Marc Boxer as editor. He briefed the artist Alan Aldridge, a fellow member of the Snowdon set, to paint the car psychedelic, a totemic Sixties word which broadly meant mind-expanding and was usually linked with hallucinogenic drugs. In painting terms it translated into vivid colours, flowing lines and strange mixtures of people, animals, flowers and unexpected objects in dreamy settings. Armed with more than a hundred tubes of gouache and six cans of silver spray paint, Aldridge first whitewashed the car and then did his stuff. I met him late in 2008, when the Design Centre in London held an exhibition of his life's work, and he described one spooky influence: the 'picture man' who went from door to door in East London when Aldridge was a boy, just after the Second World War. 'It's for the child, mum, it's for the child,' Alan recalled the tramplike figure saying, after knocking on the family's backyard door and persuading Mrs Aldridge to pay threepence for his magic lantern show. He then showed the little boy a series of brightly coloured glass slides of distant and exotic lands. They stayed in Aldridge's head and re-emerged on his painted Mini.

'Where is it now?' I asked ignorantly, assuming that the Getty or some similarly wealthy establishment would have this icon of flower power days. 'Now? It hasn't been any-where for forty-four years,' he answered sadly. 'I had to clean it off straight after the photoshoot.' The car-hire company wanted their original Mini back in its everyday livery; a sad miscalculation. If they had kept it psychedelic, they would have made a lot of money in due course. Instead Aldridge spent an afternoon soaping and scrubbing off his beautiful design. The Mini lives on only as an image, an illustration in hundreds of books and now vastly blown up and hung on the wall in the Design Centre. But it has a successor, also by Aldridge, as you will discover in due course.

One-offs like Aldridge's were the individual end of a Mini-glorifying business which was highly organised at the other. During the 1950s, a London coachbuilding company called Harold Radford's built a reputation for converting Rolls Royces and Bentleys to very high standards; they surprised the 1957 Motor Show at Earls Court with a Bentley equipped with a pull-out picnic table, hot-and-cold-water washing-up basin and expresso machine. This was a tradition with cars whose owners had almost always been extremely wealthy, going back to one owned by a million-aire in Calcutta which quacked every now and then and laid a metal egg. Harold Radford himself was an ideal operator in this field. A hunting enthusiast who had got bored with his family's shipping business after Cambridge University, he organised transport for spies during the war. His firm was lively and entrepreneurial, and its directors soon recognised that the Mini was becoming a plaything of the rich. Radford read a quip in *The Motor* that 'provided you already have a Mini, a Rolls Royce Silver Cloud makes an ideal second car', and he took action accordingly.

In 1963, his company announced three Mini conversions called collectively Mini de Villes, and individually, grandly, the De Luxe, the Bel Air and the Grande Luxe. They were crammed with the extras Issigonis deplored, and although many of these were normal in other ordinary cars – radio, cigar-lighter and foglamp, for example – the Radford versions were several steps up, drawing on the company's upmarket coachbuilding past. Their sun roofs were the same as those used in Rolls Royces and the standard colours offered were two-tone Rolls Royce livery, the colours separated by a very fine coachline ('although,' the company's onine history notes dryly, 'some of the customers' colour choices turned out to be very odd indeed'). Mini de Villes were advertised in a brochure whose cover showed a butler-like figure towering over the passenger door with the words 'Your town car, sir', while inside the specifications were summed up as 'the most luxurious small car every offered for prestige motoring in busy town traffic'.

Radford's customers included Lennon, McCartney and Harrison (Ringo went instead for their main rival Hooper's of Park Royal in London, whose Rolls Royce customers included the president of Portugal and King Paul of Greece). Radford was soon encouraged to produce a Mark 2 range. The relative opulence of the cars meant that they were slightly wider than the standard Mini, taking an early step towards today's new MINI. But they were also quieter and a lot more comfortable. Their brochure knew its psychology: the Mark 2 was 'for people who have cast envious glances at overtaking Minis, but who demand an *individual* car'. The apogee seemed to have been reached by a conversion for Mike Nesmith of The Monkees, whose £3,640 car (£55,267 today) with an astonishing nine dials on the usually rudimentary instrument panel was the most expensive Radford made. But the staying power of the car as a fashion accessory had many years to run. As recently as August 2008, a French entrepreneur based in Kensington, Jacques Blanc, was offering classic Minis with gold leaf on their bodywork, starting at £12,500. His other lines were Bentley, Porsche, Mercedes and Aston Martin.

Alongside these spectacular conversions, Radford's ran a clever off-the-peg version of each grade of the Mini de Ville and the Mark 2. It contradicted the *individual* theme of their advertising to an extent, but the market was small enough for customers still to feel that they were getting something special. Under its terms, an ordinary Mini could be customised into a De Luxe for £87 (£1,364) or a Bel Air for £223 (£3,497). The latter ended the Issigonis–Snowdon argument over sliding or wind-up windows by offering electric ones. But luxury brought problems with it. The

Radfords' deep pile carpets sometimes wedged under the pedals, causing anxious moments for drivers accelerating or, worse, slamming down the footbrake.

The involvement of Hooper's in Mini conversions underlined the curious niche the charwoman's car had secured among customers who did not need to worry about how much money they spent. Here was a firm which had always dealt exclusively with wealthy gentlemen, from its earliest days as a shop in St James's Street supplying umbrellas and leather goods to customers who were buying their hats from Lock's and wine from Berry Brothers & Rudd, who weighed customers (and still do) on a set of jumbo coffee scales as a diversion while they waited for their orders. The address had cachet but Hooper's were doubly fortunate, given the 'classless' image of the Mini, that their original factory was on that epicentre of 1960s Swinging London, the King's Road in Chelsea. Here and at the main Art Deco works in Park Royal, wonderfully skilful construction had always taken place, including the first use in cars of resin-bonded plywood, which the firm fitted into the lightweight wartime Mosquito fighter-bomber.

Hooper Minis are rare but the company had a major secondary influence on the market through two of its craftsmen, Bill Wood and Les Pickett, who left to set up their own company, also in Park Royal. They produced a rival to the Mini de Villes with the equally posh-sounding name of the Margrave, which they filled with an interior decorator's fantasy world of everything from walnut to Dralon. Customers were then offered a long list of optional extras, which struck directly at the 'make my Mini different' market which Radford's had stimulated. Battle was joined and Wood and Pickett won; in 1966 they poached not just Radford's managing director Len Minshull but also his marketing director Eddie Collins. When Harold Radford wanted a luxury upgrade for his own Triumph 1300 the following year, he took it to Wood & Pickett's rather than his own firm. They still thrive.

These eye-catching super-Minis and the fame of many of their owners had another result which gave Issigonis great satisfaction, and rightly so. To give a new word to the language is one of the clearest testimonies to the significance of a person or an event. From the first day I thought about this book, I had wondered whether the Mini was an example of this. Its origin, of course, is the Latin *minimus*, or 'very small'; but was the car responsible for 'mini' entering into general English use? Or was Issigonis beaten to it by the skirt, or even the bar? There was a clue in another quip about the Mini by Peter Sellers, that he was specially fond of it 'because it led to the miniskirt'. But could a comedian, even such a brilliant one, be trusted? There was one authoritative way to find out.

Over the years I have had a lot of dealings as a journalist with the *Oxford English Dictionary*, whose press officer Juliet Evans has a skilful way of turning the development of language into entertaining stories. She tipped me off about the book's final acceptance in 2007 of 'Jaffa cake' as a term, an event which attracted more readers' inquiries than usual because I referred in passing to the fact that *OED*'s sleuths had uncovered a small sub-cultural use of the phrase in bondage sex. We also co-operated on the dictionary's survey of euphemisms which have a known coiner – a very rare group of words and phrases, of which the most famous is probably 'wardrobe malfunction', used by Justin Timberlake to explain the exposure of his fellow-performer Janet Jackson's right breast at the Superbowl in Houston in 2004.

And so one morning in May 2009, after inspecting the Mini children's playroom at the Lord Nuffield Club in Cowley and touring the MINI works, I found myself having lunch with Juliet and the dictionary's senior editor, John Simpson. We were only a step away from the Oxford University Press's imposing headquarters on Great Clarendon Street, and John had brought a large brown package, bulging with printouts of data on word derivations and 'first sightings'. Although internet search engines have come to play a major part in such detective work, the dictionary still has thousands of enthusiasts and voluntary word-spotters who send in examples of what they consider to be new words, or old ones newly used.

Leafing through sheet after sheet, John showed me how he had stalked 'mini' back through both recent computer records and these instances sent in by readers, the latter going back for 150 years. He was surprised at how recent its coining was. A comparator, he explained after we had ordered spaghetti, was the term 'micro', as used in generic descriptions of bubble cars, which comes from the Ancient Greek *micros*, meaning small. But 'micro' as a prefix has a much longer pedigree, going back to the first experimental microscopes in the sixteenth century. Not until 1917 did 'mini' makes its debut as a prefix with the word 'minimax', a mathematical term used in problem-solving theory, followed two years later by 'minimeter', an engineering measurement device.

It was easy to get distracted, as John warmed to his subject and our forgotten pasta began to cool. Further printouts had spilled from the online dictionary's store, recording minipiano in 1934 and minicam as a noun in 1936 and a verb the following year. But the evidence I was hoping for was there just a few pages later. 'The prefix was relatively uncommon until the late 1950s,' John explained. 'And then it took off.' He pulled out another page and there it was: 'mini' as a word on its own, for the first time, in black and white. It appears in the dictionary's annual update for 1960, published less than a year after the car's launch. Then the floodgates opened. It was followed by a plethora of minithings: minicab, minibike, minimarket and only then miniskirt, first picked up by the dictionary's monitors as late as 1965.

The dictionary is careful to provide exact provenances for words, and its first sighting of Mini was in *Autocar* magazine (the researchers in Great Clarendon Street had wide-reaching radar well before the era of Google). It was used in an article on 28 August 1959. The dictionary's current online entry lists many subsequent examples, ending with an appropriate remark to the *Western Daily Press* in 2000, the last year of Mini production, by Steve Robertson, then the marketing director of Rover Group: 'The Mini has been at

Egg on rollerskates or teardrop in the wind? Names didn't hurt BMW's Isetta micro car whose success in the 1950s prompted BMC to think small. *Getty Images*

Sir Alec Issigonis, the Mini's creator, made hundreds of sketches as his brainwave developed, some in Arclight A3 tracing pads like this, others on tablecloths, napkins and the factory floor. *Rex Features*

## 1957-1959

### A REVOLUTION IN DRIVELINE ENGINEERING AND PASSENGER CAR DESIGN

Hardy Spicer

BILL CULL,
Technical Director,
Hardy Spicer Ltd.

ALEC ISSIGONIS,
Chief Engineer,
British Motor Corporation.

A very rare example of anyone getting equal billing with 'Aragonis'. Bill Cull and his special joint are given their due in a Hardy Spicer brochure.

Revealing the magic: a Mini cut in half at an Earl's Court Motor Show, reveals how tucking away the engine and boot allowed passengers 60 percent of the overall space. *Alamy*

'You've built a racing car!' John Cooper's reaction to Issigonis when he saw trial Minis hurtle round the Army's test track at Chobham, Surrey, at the car's press launch in 1959. *Rex Features*

The Mini van was one of motoring history's great bargains. Already underpriced to match Ford's cheapest car, the Mini without rear windows and passenger seats avoided purchase tax as well. *Rex Features*

The Riley Elf was one of many variants, tweaking Issigonis' design to his private alarm, but aimed at – and attracting – women drivers, with BMC adverts such as this. *Getty Images*

Mini Travellers were among the first targets for customising, a mania which saw camper vans, stretch limos and mobile burger bars crammed into that legendary tight space. *Rex Features*

Manchester United star George Best is given safe, but cramped, passage from the city's magistrates' court in 1973 after a conditional discharge for drunkenly assaulting a young woman. *Denis Thorpe*

John Cooper, the genial genius behind the fastest and most famous Minis of them all. *Rex Features*

Still Moke-ing on. The coolest of the Mini's many variants was too low slung for armies, but a must for celebs such as US talk show host David Letterman, seen here grocery shopping in 2007. *Rex Features*

Mary Quant stays loyal to the Mini after 50 years – launching a 2009 set of Royal Mail stamps which included the car and the miniskirt in a Top Ten of 20th century British design icons.   *PA Photos*

World beater. The plucky little Cooper which sped Paddy Hopkirk and Henry Liddon (pictured either side) to triumph in the 1964 Monte Carlo Rally, walloping scores of larger cars.   *Rex Features*

Actor and comedian Peter Sellers springs an expensive surprise in 1965 on his wife Britt Ekland, a Radford Mini De Ville GT with a one-off hatchback conversion. *Corbis*

The First Family of early Minis. Princess Margaret heads for her car with three-year-old Lord Linley, on their way home to Lord Snowdon after an ear operation at Great Ormond Street children's hospital, 1965. *TopFoto*

John Lennon takes a ride in fellow-Beatle George Harrison's customised and psychedelic Mini, complete with cobra curling round the petrol cap, in 1967. *Rex Features*

Twin symbols of the Sixties: 19-year-old model Twiggy at the wheel of her jazzed-up Mini – wind-up windows and a very busy dashboard – after passing her driving test in 1968. *Getty Images*

*The Italian Job*'s most celebrated stunt, the Minis' 60ft flying leap between buildings at 70mph, took place at a factory generously loaned by rivals Fiat. One car broke its suspension on landing, another its engine. *Alamy*

Metropolitan Police accident specialists examine the wreckage of the Mini in wh singer Marc Bolan of T-Rex died in 1977. His wife, American singer Gloria Jone was driving late at night in London when the car left th road and hit a tree. *Corbis*

Stephen Waldorf's Mini abandoned in Pembroke Rc Earl's Court, London in 1983, after the film editor v mistaken for escaped criminal David Martin and s five times in a traffic jam by police. *Rex Featu*

The furthest-flung Mini of all. Designed in Melbourne's Sunsh suburb, a six-wheeled Mini-trac with caterpillar tracks service Australia's Wilkes base in Antarctica in 1965.

One of mar claimants to the title of World's Shortest Mi is put throu its paces at rally in the Netherland in 1989. *Rex Feature*

Cramming women into a Mini is a major sport. This squash at Chelsea in London in 1984 was beaten by 18 Reading Ladies Rugby players in 2000 and the current holders from Malyasia's International Technical College, who managed an incredible 21 in 2006. *Rex Features*

Singer Lulu, a Sixties Mini driver, joined staff at Longbridge in October 2000 as the last – and 5,387,862nd – classic Mini left the assembly line to the strains of the theme from *The Italian Job*. *Rex Features*

Model Kate Moss, freshly through her driving test in 2001, spent an agonising ten minutes watched by paparazzi as she tried to park her Mini in Notting Hill, London. *Rex Features*

Damien Hirst's 'London Spot Mini', painted as a charity fundraiser, caused a furore in 2003 when Charles Saatchi exhibited it centre stage at his new gallery in London's former County Hall. *Rex Features*

Style guru Donatella Versace launches her one-off MINI cabriolet with a fiery flower pattern in 2005 at the charity Life Ball in Vienna town hall. It was auctioned on eBay for £105,276. *Rex Features*

Chelsea and Ivory Coast football star Didier Drogba returns to his MINI Cooper in 2008 to find that London parking wardens have got there first. *Rex Features*

Alan Aldridge's iconic painted Mini, washed clean after only three days in 1965, had this MINI successor in 2008 when a tribute exhibition at London's Design Museum also featured a lifesize copy of the Sixties original. *Rex Features*

Happy Birthday! The International Mini Meet at Birmingham in August 2009 brought cars from all over the world. Note the green Mr Bean model in the front row, complete with padlocked driver's door.

the centre of small-car culture for forty years and is loved by generations of fans.'

Why had 'mini' taken so long to reach the language? John speculated that, like the car, it was part of the twentieth century's growing ability to make things smaller; the world of the computer as against that of the steam engine in the nineteenth century. 'There was also the minimalist movement in art,' he pondered, which might be linked to Issigonis' austere rejection of everything unnecessary in his new car. There had been diminutives earlier, of course, but they had tended to be suffixes, such as manikin or yearling. The shrinking down, the cleverness at making something small but still effective or powerful, was not important enough to go at the front.

And the skirt? Not only did it come second, as John's records proved beyond challenge, but it was also created not just because of *the* Mini, but thanks to a particular car: that belonging to Mary Quant. Other fashion designers came up with 'miniskirt' at around the same time, in the way that new inventions or usages are often the product of a social trend rather than individual inspiration; but the *Oxford English Dictionary*'s earliest entry is the term 'miniskirt' on text by a picture of a leggy Quant model. There was a Mini there too, Quant's latest – and what kind was it? It was a Cooper, a name which was now to play its part in establishing the car's growing fame.

## Chapter Seven
# Super Cooper

*'A car of delightful Jekyll and Hyde character.'*
The Motor, 1963

 FORTY-SIX YEARS AGO, police and ambulance crews were called to a horrendous crash on the Kingston bypass in Surrey, where a car had clipped the kerb and somersaulted into the central reservation at an estimated 100mph. The emergency teams concentrated on getting the driver out of the wreckage, but they could hardly have failed to be astonished by his car. It was a Mini, but like no other. Instead of a rear seat, it had a second engine, linked to the one in the front by a common gearing system, part of which had gone awry and sent the car spinning out of control.

This was a Twini, an experimental nightmare which a layman could see only as an invitation to disaster at high speed. But the crash victim, whose injuries were fortunately less severe than the fractured skull at first suspected, was no layman. He was John Cooper, who together with his father Charlie transformed grand prix motor-racing in the 1950s and became a national hero in the process. When he flew off the Kingston road in 1963 he was at the start of his second great claim on his country's affection: a visionary devotion to fine-tuning the Mini which was to make its name all over the world.

'The Mini Cooper is small and mighty and I love it,' says a note from a schoolgirl called Chloe Greenall on the wall of postcard tributes to the Mini at the Heritage Motor Museum in Gaydon, and at the age of eleven she has summed up the Cooper Effect. The fashionable world had taken up the Mini, to Alec Issigonis' surprise and delight. Now it was the turn of the fast set. Chloe's parents were her age when work started on the Mini Cooper, the legendary adaptation of the standard car by John Cooper, whose initial reaction to the strange little newcomer in 1959 had been to say of Issigonis: 'This man's a bit of a comedian.'

Cooper revised that view rapidly after watching Minis cornering at speed, and seeing how the car's low centre of gravity and widely spaced wheels gave it exceptional stability. Then he was lent a pre-production model by BMC to drive to the Italian Grand Prix in Monza, the same Austin Se7en which so impressed Aurelio Lampredi of Ferrari when he took it out for a spin. Cooper heard on the grapevine too about Stirling Moss's experiences with another Longbridge car on a run around the Lickey Hills. Moss was Britain's best-known racing driver at the time, and, with the new baby's sales flagging, BMC was only too pleased to let him try out a car when he rang expressing an interest. He came back an hour later with the Mini still running but scarcely recognisable; its bonnet had been stove in and the engine section twisted in a head-on crash. Issigonis didn't mind; he told Moss that the unusually severe test drive bore out his belief that a transverse engine was less likely to shunt back into the driver. As for Moss, he got a taste of Mini power which soon brought him back for more – perhaps ill-advisedly. He was one of the first drivers of the car to be prosecuted for speeding, after police caught him overtaking another car at 90mph in Shropshire in September 1959. He was banned for a year.

Cooper was thirty-six in 1959 but already had a formidable pedigree in the racing world, not only for energetic reform and expansion of the Formula system, but as a designer of astonishingly fast cars. He had known of Issigonis' skill for years, and liked what he knew. As early as 1935, when he was an apprentice at Rootes Group, he picked up rumours about the development of the Lightweight Special, and he relished outpacing it during the late 1940s when Cooper cars dominated the sprint and hill-climb field. Regularly the Lightweight came up against the Cooper 500, and lost to it. That could have soured relations between the rival drivers, but Issigonis' pride was not affronted. He recognised a fellow devotee and an exceptionally skilled one; and he just liked Cooper, as everyone did.

Genial, amusing and a devoted pipe smoker, the young engineer had a winning combination of nonchalance and flair. On the day of the near-disaster at Kingston, he had given some friends a lift in his Tri-Pacer light aircraft to an aerobatic display at Biggin Hill and was about to take off for home, when one of his passengers asked him: 'Isn't it the form to inspect the plane before you fly, John?' This was a polite way of pointing out that the plane's tail was bent, after someone had hit it while taxi-ing and, as happens in the more mundane world of supermarket car parks, failed to leave a note. Cooper recalled wryly in his autobiography that the Tri-pacer had only just been repaired following a cartwheeling crash, and that the borrowed plane which took the Biggin Hill party home instead had a newly qualified pilot who got lost and flew in a ham-fisted way which terrified everyone on board. When they landed and parted company, Cooper tore off in the Twini to get home in time for supper with his wife Pauline. He lived life at high speed.

The disastrous Twini, with its wildly disproportionate 2.5 litre engine, four-wheel drive and individual wheelspin, was nonetheless typical of the imagination and practical know-how which lay behind Cooper's success. He was commercially talented – as we have seen, he owned his own aircraft before he was forty – due in part to a partnership with his equally formidable father. Charlie Cooper ran a dark and clutter-filled garage in Surbiton between the wars, winning the loyalty of underpaid and often grumbling mechanics by his drive, complete mastery of fast car engines and a procession of interesting and distinguished customers. The grubby workshop was close to Brooklands racing circuit and Cooper developed particular links with the motor-racing champion Kaye Don, working on the Irishman's Sunbeams Tiger, Tigress and Cub and a Wolseley Viper which took the Brooklands lap record to 137.58mph. Racing ace and mechanical expert got on well together, and Don had a laid-back style which may have influenced the character of Charlie's son.

Summing up his way of life, which included flipping a world-record speedboat and a four-month jail term for manslaughter after a crash on the Isle of Man which killed his co-driver, he mused: 'One or two experiences that I have had have been somewhat thrilling.'

John Cooper had the run of the garage and in due course took an apprenticeship with his father before joining a specialised tool-making company which did secret work for the Admiralty during the Second World War. Very high performance levels were required in a field which at around this time was to see the first use of Bill Cull's increasingly clever continuous velocity joints in submarine conning towers. Cooper loved it, and when the war ended he was eager to manage something similar of his own. His father was well aware of John's skills and thought that they would work well with his own commercial nous, which had seen the Surbiton business expand into a small chain of companies. He suggested that they go into business together, making lightweight racing cars to meet the demand for excitement and fun which had returned with peace.

The Cooper Car Company was the result, the forerunner of the great string of British motor-racing names which emerged from the 1950s onwards, and it soon dominated the home market. As well as building exceptional racing cars, the Coopers set up their own racing team, featuring drivers such as Stirling Moss, his Australian rival Jack Brabham and the young Mike Hawthorn. John Cooper's skilful engineering made the Cooper Climax series of cars as rapid as the more powerful but heavier Ferraris which regarded grand prix victories as theirs by right. They were also a lot nippier. The key was a bold reshaping of traditional engineering: just as Issigonis revolutionised small car design with the Mini's transverse, front-wheel-drive engine, John Cooper pioneered racing cars with the engine behind the driver. The change from front-mounted engines transformed handling and road-holding and was soon copied by everyone else.

Cooper was thus a respected name in motor-racing circles in 1959, and fortuitously he had renewed his dealings with Issigonis earlier in the year, while looking for a new engine for his latest cars. The negotiations with BMC did not go well, but Cooper took the chance of dropping in on the Mini project and looking closely at the new car. After the launch and his trip to Monza in the Austin Se7en, he began to think about the completely unexpected: could a souped-up version of this small, strange but brilliantly engineered saloon actually *be* his new racer?

He had been foreshadowed by a prophetic article in *Motor Sport* as early as September 1959, immediately after the launch of the two cars at Longbridge and Cowley, which asked: '*What* have these new small cars to do with enthusiasts?' and immediately provided the answer: 'Ask the firms that are even now tuning and modifying them for high speed.' These included the Downton Engineering Works, based near Salisbury, whose owner Daniel Richmond had a legendary reputation for 'improving' cars, including Bentleys, Lagondas and Rolls Royces. Rumoured to clean out engines with gin, he was offering a go-faster kit for the Mini costing £33 (£574) within three months of the launch.

The same piece speculated that the arrival of Issigonis' new creation — whose technical wizardry appealed to the magazine's specialist writers and readers if not yet to the mass market — might lead 'some enterprising organiser to stage a race for babies'.

It wasn't a race just for babies which Cooper had in mind when he went to see Issigonis again towards the end of 1960. The pair had a decisive conversation, which the designer recalled in a BBC interview for his eightieth birthday. Describing the Mini as both 'a little family car' and 'fantastic', Cooper asked Issigonis if he had taken it round a racing circuit. 'No, should I have done?' Issigonis replied. 'It's a people's car, I built it for them to go shopping and on holiday.' He was game-playing; his own company's launch films had shown the trial cars scorching up snow-covered hairpins in the Alps and cornering comfortably at 50mph on Spanish gravel.

Cooper pushed the point home: 'You haven't built a people's car, you've built a racing car. We ought to build some for the boys, you know, a little bit better, bit more steam ...' Issigonis played dubious for a little longer, but then decided: 'We ought to go and see the headmaster' – in other words seek permission from Leonard Lord and George Harriman. This was given, and Cooper went off with the mission of turning a sheep, the nippy but modest standard Mini, into a wolf.

He had been encouraged by the fact that some of the Climax drivers, including Jack Brabham and Bruce McLaren, had bought their own Minis and adjusted their engines – a racing-circuit version of the Radford and Hooper transformations commissioned by celebrity Mini owners, for style rather than speed. The key was the fact that the Mini's A Series engine ran well at much higher ratings than the official 850cc. The original Mini Project had reduced power from 948cc in test vehicles in a fit of alarm after one turned over and the whole car was reckoned to be too powerful and fast. Modified A Series engines had also achieved great things for Morris Minors and Austin A35s and A40s on rally circuits and race tracks. Throughout 1960 assorted examples of beefed-up Minis careered around tracks from Brands Hatch, where one had the crowd on its feet by overtaking the winner of the 2.6 litre class, to the Monte Carlo Rally. In their first attempt on this Everest of motor sport, a Mini managed twenty-third place, with three others coming in at thirty-third, fifty-fifth and seventy-third after mechanical problems and a roll-over.

The BMC competitions department added some to its race and rally fleet, but not with any enthusiasm. The works foreman there, Doug Watts, refused to drive down to the bank in one, because he did not want to be seen by friends in such an insignificant-looking car. He was already out of date. Ordinary owners as well as the experts at Downton were vying with one another to soup up the most modest Minis. A typical recollection was pinned to the Mini card wall of visitors' memories at the Motor Heritage Museum this year. Christopher Kingsley wrote down how his uncle took him along on drives as a sort of 'speed assistant'. His job was to operate a home-made fuel injection system made up of a bottle of washing-up liquid taped to the car's controls. Every couple of minutes, Christopher was asked to squeeze, and the Mini bucked into an even faster speed.

Cooper's own conversion, working miracles with twin carburettors, a modified cylinder head and new camshaft as well as the rebored engine, was to supercede all this. Within months he was back in Harriman's office with a 997cc engine created from these changes, plus disc brakes and new gears installed in the car. Parked outside the Kremlin at Longbridge and painted the signature red of the marque, it was the first of the famous Mini Cooper brand.

Cooper had to fight to get Harriman to agree to make 1000 models of the car, the minimum requirement for entrants in the new Formula Junior championship which the Mini Cooper was targeting. With the help of Issigonis, who tried out the experimental car at Silverstone and was impressed, he overcame Harriman's doubts that so many could be sold. As well as his engineering skill, he also offered permanent use of the Cooper name, the most sought-after brand in British motor-racing at the time, in return for a £2 royalty (£33 today) on each car. After muddles, a resurgence of the old rivalry between Austin and Morris and the brief nightmare that the notorious Mini water leaks might drown the project (a trial Cooper was squirted with a powerful hose from all angles), the wolf was ready for release in July 1961. The launch was attended by twenty-seven Grand Prix drivers including Moss, Brabham, McLaren and Graham Hill and was a triumph. Now the racing had to begin.

The Cooper's arrival coincided with an energetic new regime at the competitions department which BMC had built up in the old MG sports car headquarters at Abingdon, a short drive from Cowley. Stuart Turner was still in his twenties and his youthful enthusiasm worked well with old hands in a team which had seen plenty of glory days not just with MGs, but using less likely cars such as the Morris Minor. In the hands of Stirling Moss's sister Pat, whose horse-racing fame gave BMC both its rosette symbol and the title of 'ecurie', or stable, for its racing team, the outwardly cosy moggy had triumphed in several European rallies. Turner himself had been on some of them as one of the team's most guileful navigators, including an outing with Pat Moss in the first-ever rally in which a Mini took part. This was a small Shropshire club meet called the Knowledale Car Club Mini Miglia held in November 1959, only three months after the Mini's launch. The entry car TJB 199 was 'rather slow, a new model and had never been rallied before', said Moss, but she and Turner won by ten minutes; a portent of things to come.

Now it was the Mini Cooper's turn and in 1962 the car was entered both for rallies and racetrack events, BMC dealing with the former while the Cooper Car Company built on their formidable expertise on the track. Cups and First Prize rosettes came swiftly: Pat Moss won the Dutch Tulip rally in a Cooper in May and the car topped a series of successful track appearances by taking the national saloon car trophy of the British Racing and Sports Car Club in September. Its tally for the year reached 153 trophies or placings, ranking just ahead of the mighty Mercedes Benz in terms of championship and class results. Then in January 1963, as snow fell over much of Europe, the little cars entered the world's biggest rally, sliding and speeding their way to Monte Carlo. Some spectators laughed initially, but one car driven by the Finn Raunoa Aaltonen came third, with Paddy Hopkirk just behind on fourth. These achievements were a prelude to greater glory.

Issigonis was a natural racing-car enthusiast, with years of competing in his Lightweight Special behind him, but he was still cautious about how well the Coopers would ultimately do. His scepticism finally vanished when he had lunch with the BBC anchorman Cliff Michelmore at his favourite pub in Oxford, the Trout on the Thames at Godstow, in the summer of 1963. A Mini Cooper driven by Paddy Hopkirk was competing in the Tour de France rally and Michelmore casually mentioned, at the end of an interview about other motoring issues, that he looked bound to win. Issigonis, distracted by design responsibilities at BMC, was surprised, but he checked and discovered that Hopkirk was indeed in the lead. Within twenty-four hours Issigonis was in Monaco to watch the final lap – with the boost of an extra £15 beyond the then tight restrictions on taking currency abroad. A bank clerk dealing with the last-minute transaction was a Mini owner and recognised Issigonis' name.

Hopkirk duly triumphed in 33 EJB, sweeping past Issigonis, who was jumping up and down and shouting at him not to drive too close to a Jaguar in front, because the handicap system had already guaranteed the Cooper first place. There was much celebrating in the little principality, and naturally discussions about the coming 'Monte' in January 1964. The team was now racing with the new and more powerful Mini Cooper S, whose 1071cc engine soon saw another cup added to the Abingdon shelf when Warwick Banks won the European Touring Car Championship. Intensive practice took place and Issigonis spared nothing and no one as the January start-date drew near. Stuart Turner called in at Longbridge in October with a shopping list of extras for the rally cars and was amazed at how senior engineers scurried off – literally running – in response to Issigonis' insistence that every demand from Abingdon be met at once. Interviewed for Gillian Bardsley's official biography of Issigonis, he recalled: 'I got the feeling at the time that if I'd gone up there and said, "I'm sorry Alec but the competition team have decided we've got to have purple-striped rear windows on every Mini that's ever sold," he'd have said, "Yes dear boy, yes," and someone would have been buzzed in and purple-striped rear windows would have been put in.'

Paddy Hopkirk won the Monte. The public and media reaction was instructive for BMC's marketing people. Giant-killing by the little car which was becoming a symbol of Sixties Britain, stylish, fun and with a cheeky ability to beat the odds, was a story that everyone wanted. Hopkirk's Mini was photographed with the Beatles in Paris and then flown to London, where it topped the bill at Bruce Forsyth's show *Saturday Night at the London Palladium*. Flanked by Hopkirk and his team, the car revolved on a dais while Tiller

Girls high-kicked through a dance routine, Forsyth and Tommy Cooper cracked jokes and Kathy Kirby sang. The sell-out audience sang too, belting out *Rule Britannia* before the curtain came down.

John Cooper meanwhile went back to his engine-boring machines, after persuading BMC to take the little car up to 1275cc, quite a trick to turn with an engine originally designed to run at 803cc. He succeeded, and the following year the razzamatazz was renewed when Mini Cooper won the rally again, this time with Timo Makinen, another 'flying Finn', driving the successful car. And then came the greatest publicity booster of all. In the 1966 Monte Carlo Rally, Mini Coopers took a hat-trick – first, second and third – only to be disqualified for using supposedly illegal lights. The decision caused uproar in Britain and was widely denounced as a French plot. Jealousy of the gutsy little invaders had revived all the old animosities between Frog and Perfidious Albion, the theory went, bolstered by the fact that a Citroën took the trophy, although its driver Henri Toivonen sportingly admitted that his victory was 'hollow'. The Mini team were initially downcast and cancelled flights back home for another and even more spectacular celebration. But they had reckoned without the way the media and public relations work. Minis winning the Monte Carlo and scooping the top three slots would have been a big story; Minis winning and being disqualified was huge. The flights were restored and this time the London Palladium curtain went up on the three rally cars circling a darkened stage with their illegal lights shining. The show's host Jimmy

Tarbuck eventually stopped Makinen, who had driven the winning Mini, and asked him: 'Did you really need those lights?' To thunderous applause, the Finn replied: 'I could have won it with a bunch of glow-worms on the front.'

The Coopers sealed their astonishing run of Monte victories with a final triumph in 1967, after a nail-bitingly close finish which saw the team go to bed still uncertain of the result and convinced that they had just lost. It was a pleasant reward after the previous year's disqualification, but Abingdon also knew that faster and more sophisticated rivals were certain to take their little car's place in 1968. The triumphant trio from 1966 were kept in good order back at the Competitions Department and in due course passed to the Motor Heritage Centre in Gaydon, where they form a centrepiece of the huge display. Driving for ever on a tilting dais which gives the impression of the ups and downs of the Monte Carlo rally, the little red-and-white convoy still takes people's breath away. Such a small car. Such a big rally. Such a long way. That was how thousands of enthusiasts felt at the time, and it showed in Mini sales.

Not everyone could afford a Cooper, any more than the ordinary motorist was likely to go for a Radford Mini de Ville Grand Luxe. There were also plenty of parents who baulked at the insurance and the thought of their offspring careering around in an oversized go-kart with an engine fit for a racing car. But sales went up by just over half for the Mini and a little over a third for the Mini Cooper in the first quarter of 1964, following Hopkirk's Monte victory, compared with the same three months the year before.

Dealers in Belgium and particularly France reported a surge in interest, and Hopkirk told *Autosport* years later: 'The car became very fashionable – I mean it was more impressive to pick your girlfriend up in Paris in a Mini than in an E-type Jag.' The fact that the car retained its modest look, with only red-and-white or green-and-white livery plus discreet signing and badging distinguishing it from ordinary Minis, was the essence of 1960s cool.

Advertising for other cars in the Mini range picked up on the heroics, particularly a series of spoof historical adventures which you can watch at the Motor Heritage Museum. They start with mediaeval knights jousting astride cars rather than carthorses, with the Mini triumphing after the rival car in the lists shoots off leaving its metal-clad jockey dangling. Then comes a Battle of Britain clip with a heavily moustached Biggles figure leading a squadron of white-painted Minis, with RAF roundels on their sides and roof, in pursuit of Ford Anglias bearing German air-force Maltese crosses. After cross-hairs appear on the boot of an Anglia, smoke spurts from its stricken innards to the sound of suitably breakdown-themed music, and it veers off and staggers to a halt. Grinning and doing a thumbs-up, the Mini 'pilot' sticks another 'Ford' label on his list of 'kills' on the Mini's front wing, and heads off to battle again, twitching his eyebrows up and down in anticipation.

The commercial value of the racing success was registered in sales after each victory, and from the start. Hopkirk's success in the 1963 Tour de France meant that during the race his little car was seen thrashing much bigger rivals such as the Ford Falcons for some twenty minutes a day on French TV. More than 10,000 Mini Coopers were made in the car's first year and just over 100,000 in ten years. But a decade was all that the original, and most glorious Coopers, got.

Their fans still talk incredulously today about how the supercars became the victim of wider events, as the unhappy state of BMC's finances led the firm into merger talks and, in early 1968, a one-sided marriage to the much stronger company British Leyland. Headed by Donald Stokes, whose youthful (and lasting) enthusiasm for buses did not bode well for very small cars, British Leyland added new unhappinesses to the old Austin–Morris tensions which had plagued BMC throughout its life. Existing staff had to accommodate the new ways of incomers from Standard Triumph, old rivals who were part of Leyland. Stokes' executives such as Filmer Paradise, a cigar enthusiast from Oregon who was put in charge of sales, made no secret of their admiration for the tighter and harsher management of Ford, and new recruits were poached whenever possible from Dagenham.

Stokes was not enthusiastic about the Mini in general, which he regarded as an ageing car, but its hold on public affection was by now so strong that he agreed to further improvements and the standardising of all the variants, such as the Riley Elf and Wolseley Hornet, under the single, simple name of Mini from 1969. But he had his sights on the Cooper, and he took aim and fired in 1971 after meeting John Cooper following the merger and asking him what he did. The easy-going Cooper did not have the measure of the new man in charge and his jokey response – 'I win world championships and come up to Longbridge once a fortnight to wind Issigonis up' – did not amuse the ruthless business-man. After studying the finances of the Cooper and in particular the high insurance costs faced by its owners, Stokes unilaterally ended the £2 royalty agreement, which, made in the relatively gentlemanly days of Lord and Harriman, had never been written down. 'We lost about £20 per Mini,' he recalled later. 'Then people wonder why I scrapped the Cooper, but we were losing even more money on that.' The car was replaced in BMC's stable by a 1275GT Clubman, but the Cooper name disappeared as part of the divorce, and things were never the same. Stokes gained on insurance – the new car was in category four (out of ten) while the Cooper S had hit category seven. But he lost far more by losing the right to Britain's most famous motor-racing brand. It was to be more than thirty years before that blunder, another in the catalogue of Mini mistakes, was put right.

Such powerful feelings played a part in the Mini's revival as the big new MINI; but the original, extraordinarily gutsy Cooper S in its diminutive package retains its own hold eight years after the launch of BMW's successor car. Less than a mile from my home in Leeds, a 1964 rally version, built in the year that Hopkirk took 33 EJB to Monte Carlo glory, stands like a Noddy car amid the sleek, angular shapes of half a dozen Formula One racers. Even more imposing, in this stable of supercharged classics, is a Bugatti Royale the size of a small bus; not one of the six originals of this extraordinary monster created by Etienne Bugatti, which proved too expensive even for Europe's royal families during the 1930s depression, but an exact replica. Using specifications provided by the owners of the six originals, the car was built in Britain as a luxuriously expensive conceit. In an echo of Bill Cull and his workshop in Shipley, the engine was made in Batley.

The Speedmaster showrooms in Bradford where these cars are displayed are the brainchild of James Hanson, who races historic Formula One cars and European tourers. His grandfather Jack Hanson was a hill-climbing competitor in the days of Scott and similar heroes, and his interest in speed and power has been passed on. He races the cars but makes his living by selling them. If you want the rebuilt 1964 Cooper, you will need £35,000, but then consider how much history you get from that; history recorded in paintings, poetry, prose and above all, film.

## Chapter Eight
# Miniculture

 AS IF THE MINI HADN'T HAD ENOUGH in the way of fairy godmothers to make up for its faltering start, it now benefited from the talents of an imaginative TV scriptwriter called Troy Kennedy Martin. After a modest beginning writing half a dozen plays for the BBC, he made headlines in 1962 as the co-creator of *Z Cars*, which took the British police out of the cosy world of Jack Dixon and Dock Green nick, and introduced rough, tough men in big patrol cars based in Kirkby on Merseyside. They were not the type who would have driven a standard Mini, but it was not the ordinary version of the car which Kennedy Martin had in mind when he developed an offbeat idea for a crime thriller a few years later. The notion had actually come from his brother Ian Kennedy Martin, also a first-rate scriptwriter who was responsible for *The Sweeney*, another tale of hard-edged coppers in which Troy had a hand too (and which featured two safely parked Minis in episode one).

All the research for the series, and its many twists and turns in the life of London's then Flying Squad ('Sweeney Todd' in Cockney rhyming slang), had given Ian the idea of a robbery set in a traffic jam. Troy had a mind cluttered with information too, and among its many scraps of data was a description he had recently read of the new computerised traffic-control system in Turin. He liked Italy, his sister worked in Rome and Ian was happy for him to take the infant plot over and transfer it to the capital city of the Mini's great European rival, Fiat. At some stage the brothers joked about the possible reaction of Gianni Agnelli, not merely president of Fiat, but the man who controlled 4.4 per cent of Italy's gross domestic product, 3.1 per cent of its workforce and 16.5 per cent of its industrial research. Would he really appreciate an invasion of Minis?

The engaging Cockney star Michael Caine was recruited, after Ian met him during a delay to flights at Los Angeles airport. Caine won the interest of Paramount, who were looking for a new film for him following the success of *Alfie* (which had just one Mini briefly in the background when the eponymous hero was buying flowers in a London street) and his spy films based on the novels of Len Deighton (there was a pair of Minis, one red, one white, and very like the ones used in the first episode of *The Sweeney*, parked opposite a phone box in *The Ipcress File*). More negotiations followed and in the course of them the Kennedy Martin brothers' original concept of something as hard-edged as *Z Cars* or *The Sweeney* became the comic caper which the world now knows, and almost universally loves, as *The Italian Job*. Troy Kennedy

Martin, who died in September 2009, was not best pleased and later said dismissively: 'I just let them get on with it.' It was as well that they did. He had wanted a blood-soaked shootout at the end. Instead, full of one-liners and with the traditional British virtues of phlegm and a stiff upper lip transferred to the robbery gang, it saw Caine and the immortal Noël Coward at their considerable best. But they were wholly upstaged. Just as the most memorable image from Caine's first big success *Zulu* is nothing in his own fine performance as Lieutenant Gonville Bromhead but the massed, chanting, foot-stamping impis on the skyline above Rorke's Drift, so *The Italian Job* is completely stolen by its Minis. Every cliché in the marketeers' book was justified by their cheeky, perky, feisty, gutsy acrobatics down the back alleys, in the sewers and across the rooftops of Turin. Teetering close to a parody of *Zulu*, *The Great Escape* and many other films in the pantheon of heroic sagas, the cars looked like knowing innocents, a description coined by another actor, Peter Ustinov. They ran rings round the human stars and, of course, the pursuing police who, in deference to Fiat, whose own cars appear mostly as victims of the stupendous traffic jam, were given Alfa Romeo Giulias.

As it turned out, the film-makers need not have worried about Giovanni Agnelli. He loved the idea, and although his offer to supply free Fiats for the starring role was politely refused, as he knew it would be, he allowed the most famous scene in the film to be made at the Fiat factory in Lignetti on the outskirts of Turin. Employees there said formal goodbyes to the team of stunt drivers after hearing what was planned, because they were convinced that they would be killed. But what a contrast this Italian welcome was, to the response which the project received from British Leyland. In yet another of the firm's catalogue of Mini-related mistakes, the marketing department wasn't interested. Complacent about the marque's success – for by 1968, when filming started, it had captured the small-car market in Britain to an unprece-dented degree – they simply weren't bothered about Caine and Coward and their bubblingly enthusiastic, Mini-focused plan. Would they give or lease the production team any cars? They would not. Lending was perhaps a euphemism, consider-ing what Kennedy Martin's script was about to put the Minis through; but all that Longbridge eventually offered was six cars at trade cost. The remaining thirty which the film-makers needed for their destructive antics had to be bought in the same way and at the same price as ordinary punters were paying in the showrooms. Other than that, some technical help was unofficially supplied to power up a Mini which climbs a long flight of Turin steps; and the firm paid the £10 bill for Issigonis (who much enjoyed the film) to hire a Birmingham cinema for a private showing to colleagues and friends.

The curmudgeonly response could have lost the company its greatest single piece of PR for the car, as Agnelli got wind of what was happening and re-opened every door in Fiat's power. In Turin, that meant literally every door, and the city was memorably co-operative in allowing the producers to create temporary chaos. Agnelli resurrected his offer to the Paramount team of as many cars as they would like, if they wanted to switch from Minis to the smallest version of his own product line. There could be cash help too, the company suggested, and how about a complimentary Ferrari? British Leyland's name was saved not by saintliness on the crew's part, or a noble patriotism of the Rorke's Drift sort, but because the Mini was essential. The film was about British cunning, guile and (without giving away the ending in the unlikely event that you haven't seen it), irrepressible optimism. One of the best-known one-liners in the script also demanded a British car: 'Just remember,' says Caine, as his troops scramble like a dodgy RAF fighter squadron, 'in this country, they drive on the wrong side of the road.'

Perhaps Kennedy Martin took a subtle revenge in his script, when Noël Coward's character Mr Bridger, a criminal mastermind who in the best Francis Drake tradition justifies the robbery as good for Britain's balance of payments, sighs in his prison-cell headquarters about 'the lazy, unimaginative management which is driving this country on the rocks'. Fiat also got plenty of mentions throughout the film, as the £4 million in gold bars in Caine and the Minis' sights are the Chinese government's down payment for a plant designed to make Agnelli's little cars near Beijing. Michael Caine didn't bother with subtlety in a TV interview looking back on the film a decade later, commenting: 'That's why the company no longer exists and that's the problem with British industry. We hate British Leyland.'

The film poked fun elsewhere, notably at the image of well-to-do Mini owners who treated the car as a plaything. The drivers of the three Mini Coopers in the story (each a composite of twelve actual cars with a bevy of stunt drivers) were deliberately cast as toff poshers, the sort of buyers who knew

Lord Snowdon, or at least someone who had danced with him, and chose the little car partly on the grounds of style. But the marvellous chase sequences also left no doubt about what the Cooper S could do, following on from its heroics in the Monte Carlo rally, and also suggested that its owners had deep-down grit. As Caine says to his fellow gangsters when they meet Chris, Tony and Dominic and snigger at their Old Etonian accents: 'These chinless wonders will get you out of Turin faster than anyone else on four wheels. Remember that!' Other memorable lines were delivered not in Italy but inside the new Birmingham–Coventry sewer at Stoke Aldermoor in Warwickshire's Sowe Valley, which was finished but not yet in use. An office block in Twickenham also saved Paramount money by doubling as Turin's traffic-control centre.

The real-life drivers were partly professional stuntmen recruited by Remy Julienne, master of car tricks in six James Bond movies and a succession of adverts for Renault and Citroën, but they also included some of the men who had put the Mini through its paces at Issigonis' trials. Two of the crew decided to celebrate the end of filming by racing a couple of the Coopers back to England, which went well until the final lap in Essex. One of them screeched past a Chief Inspector's wife and was flagged down a few miles further on. He had several of the production team's fake gold bars still in his boot and it was a little late to explain everything. He spent that night in the cells.

*The Italian Job* has been the Mini's dominant cultural reference point for forty years, with offshoots including the annual Italian Job Rally to Turin. References to it abound in other films and TV series, and in 2008 the Royal Society of Chemistry ran a competition to highlight the centenary of the Periodic Table, in which entrants had to propose a viable solution to the quandary at the end of the film. To help the better understanding of science, this had to be practicable, thoroughly explained with relevant calculations, take no more than thirty minutes and not involve the use of a helicopter. I am not going to spoil things by reproducing the solution here, the work of John Godwin, an IT manager from Godalming in Surrey, but it is printed upside down on page 248.

The film imitated the Mini in one less happy way; although nominated for a Golden Globe as best foreign film of 1969, the year of *Butch Cassidy*, *Midnight Cowboy* and *Easy Rider*, it failed to make any headway in the United States. The real car was no icon there; it had been withdrawn from sale two years earlier because of tighter federal safety laws, and after hostile media comments. *The Italian Job* made enough of an impression with Hollywood professionals, however, to earn a remake in 2003, with Donald Sutherland taking Coward's Mr Bridger role. The Mini also benefited from that, in the form of the new MINI, which was used in its predecessor's place. There is talk of a sequel, an idea proposed for Kennedy Martin's original but dropped after the poor showing in the States.

But although the original film did not reach the dizziest heights internationally, it has since become a global phenomenon in terms of the number of societies, groups, websites and amateur forensic scientists determined to extract every nuance, every fact and rumour about its making. Is that the BBC's Crystal Palace transmitter in the background of one Mini-racing sequence? Yes. Does the red, white and blue sequence of the fleeing cars change colours en route? It does. Was there a surreal dance session between the Minis and Italian police cars filmed inside Pier Luigi Nervi's famous concrete exhibition hall with an orchestra playing *The Blue Danube*? There was, and although it was removed from the final cut, it was restored on later DVDs of the film. Another cut, taking the chase on to an ice rink, was unearthed only in 1998 by Channel Four. Yet another, of girls in their undies abseiling rather clumsily from Caine's flat when his girlfriend Lorna comes home (there were few women in the stunt trade in 1968) remained buried.

When the rock band Stereophonics made a cod video based on the film in 1999, their lead singer Kelly Jones said: 'I wouldn't trust anyone who doesn't like *The Italian Job*.' The remark hit on the way the film took the chirpy, cheeky, very post-imperial tone of Britain at the climax – and effectively the end – of the Swinging Sixties. It guyed everything, and the stories surrounding its making have continued the tradition. Fans fall about at the revelation that six black horses used in one sequence, filmed in Dublin on a filthy wet day, gradually went grey and then brown as the dye painted on by the dealer who supplied them was washed off by the rain. Later generations of British film-makers, brought up on the movie, adopted both a similar, gently witty, style and the Mini, notably Richard Curtis' *Four Weddings and a Funeral*, in which Hugh Grant and Charlotte Coleman career to the first of the weddings in a battered

Cooper S. 'It only goes at forty miles an hour,' says Coleman, with a madcap rush to Somerset in prospect. The next script direction reads: 'The tiny Cooper is speeding along the motorway at a tremendously illegal speed – definitely twice 40 miles per hour. It is shaking with the effort.' The car reappears regularly, screeching to a halt, clamped, speeding and ticketed, as the weddings progress and Grant tries vainly not to be late.

The Four Weddings Mini took a clobbering; but nothing compared to the even dirtier and more battered red Cooper which is crucial to Matt Damon and Franka Potente's escape from mysterious but definitely evil pursuers in *The Bourne Identity*. This film actually had a destruction ratio higher than the thirty-six cars used in *The Italian Job*; the producer Frank Marshall ordered five and ended up with one survivor, which was later tracked down at a studios theme park in the States by Welsh and Yorkshire hunters of interesting Minis abroad (see page 197). He wanted a Mini for similar reasons to Kennedy Martin: it was nimble and agile, ideal for skeetering down stairways and sliding down alleys in Mediterranean towns. It also appealed to the nostalgic market which bathes anything to do with the 1960s in a hazy golden glow. 'It was an old car but it was also a hip car,' he explained. 'When I was younger, it was a very cool car to have. It was my fantasy to drive one of those across Europe.'

The film also has a nerdy appeal to super-knowledgable Mini enthusiasts, because its many continuity glitches, which include a lot of coming and going of snow in supposedly connected scenes, alter the type of car during the various chases. Watch carefully, or indeed car-fully, and you will see that the steering wheel has a Cooper badge when Damon and Potente are parked in front of a Paris railway station. This then changes to a standard Mini badge during the hottest of the chase scenes, and then back to a Cooper Mini again. Who cares? No one, it just adds to the fun, as the use of Mini with a Morris badge but Austin radiator grille did during another car chase, in the Christopher Lee and Peter Cushing classic *The Satanic Rites of Dracula* in 1974. Observe also the way that the Mini's windscreen is cracked in a collision with a phone box, but then mends itself before reappearing. Batteredness, on the lines of Paddy Hopkirk's Monte Carlo-winning Cooper, is also part of the car's appeal. On it depends the success of Damon's sceptical comment as he accepts a getaway ride with Potente: 'You take good care of this car?'

Someone who did take care of his on-screen Mini, to famously excessive lengths, was Mr Bean, whose use of a lime-green 1977 model with a black bonnet is second only to *The Italian Job* in Mini cinematography. This is not only the case in Britain, where Rowan Atkinson's surreal humour strikes a familiar national chord. Foreign admirers are also everywhere, praising what the website Malaysian Mini Lover calls the comedian's knowledge of the old saying that beauty lies in the eyes of the beholder. 'It's just like Mr Bean go for the classic Mk 3 Mini,' it says, explaining to readers why Atkinson didn't opt for the latest and most powerful type of Cooper. The car's everyday nature was improved, however, by Mr Bean's paranoid security arrangements: a bolt and padlock and a starting and stopping mechanism which removed the whole steering wheel rather than the ignition key. Once again, the Mini's record of attrition in movie-making struck the Bean team. Enthusiasts will point out to you that the Mini used in episode one was orange with a black bonnet. Unfortunately, that car was wrecked in a real-life, offscreen accident. It could not be repaired, unlike a stunt double of the lime green one, which is squashed by a tank in *Back to School Mr Bean*, but reappears in later episodes.

The Bean saga ran for fourteen episodes, the first in January 1990 and the last in October 1995, and its popularity helped the Mini during its last decade, when sales were kept at a viable level by special editions, priced more dearly than the traditional off-the-peg cars, and a growing enthusiasm among young and reasonably affluent people for anything retro. Similar nudges and reminders of a car which was beginning to get pretty elderly, and had become far less frequent on Britain's roads, were given by Shane Meadows, a director cannily in touch with the country's everyday but often eccentric life. His *A Room for Romeo Brass* in 1999 gave plenty of time and space to one of the main characters' drab green Minivan, whose supremacy in the car side of things was only briefly threatened by a bright pink ice-cream van. Three years later, *Once Upon a Time in the Midlands* starred not only Robert Carlyle, Kathy Burke and Ricky Tomlinson but also a four-door stretch Mini limousine, a genre which will reappear in the next chapter, plus a yellow, Mr Bean-like saloon on top of a garage.

It might have been lifted there by the Bionic Woman, had

the films been made twenty years earlier, when Lindsay Wagner gave a Mini with the registration plate MOC 223P the hike of its life. Still managing to smile in a relaxed fashion, the series' heroine Jaime Sommers, a tennis professional reassembled bionically after a sky-diving accident, hoicked the car up effortlessly on behalf of the US government in her work for the FBI. Viewers couldn't see the crane. Car chases or nippy manoeuvres on TV were meanwhile daily bread for the Mini for all of its five decades: *The Saint*, *The Avengers*, *The Champions*, *The Persuaders*, *Heartbeat*, *Friends* (when the action moved to London) and of course *Top Gear*. It is still going strong on the small screen. When Martina Navratilova was recruited for the elimination challenge *I'm a Celebrity, Get Me Out of Here* in 2008, her finest moment came on a high-wire dash across three classic Mini Coopers. They were painted red, white and blue on *The Italian Job* lines and hung over a gorge, into which, when a timer expired, they plunged.

There was one more film to come, before the new MINI started to muscle in on Hollywood's script-writing sessions and win roles with Austin Powers and the remake of *The Italian Job*. It was very odd. How were names such as Simon Callow, Stephen Fry and even Keira Knightley persuaded to take part in *Thunderpants*, a clunky jokefest on the subject of a boy whose uncontrollable flatulence becomes the subject of a tussle between good scientists (British) and bad ones (American) who want the gas to power respectively hovercraft and space rockets? The production in 2002 died the death, although its juvenile lead Rupert Grint was praised for escaping his typecast part as Ron Weasley in the Harry Potter epics, but it had one relatively subtle, referential quip. The director Peter Hewitt made a film in 1997 of Mary Norton's classic children's story *The Borrowers*. He set it in an unidentified part of the Midlands and had everyone driving Morris Minors. In *Thunderpants*, the English all drive green Minis, while the Americans have a sinister black Lincoln Continental.

Second in Minicultural importance after its film appearances comes a curious form of art which the Mini has made its own. How many elephants can you get in a Mini? Two in the front and four in the back. How many people can you get in? Now that's a much longer and richer tale. The urge to Mini-cram dates back to the earliest days and the eye-catching launches at Longbridge and Cowley when processions of grown-ups, children, pets and belongings emerged from the very first show cars. From A-level celebrants at Greenhead high school in Huddersfield to Blue Peter presenters on BBC TV, the challenge has led to some bizarre gymnastics and muffled cries of 'I'm suffocating, get me out of here,' all of it prompting enormous interest; a Google search of 'Record number of people in a Mini' brings up 6,820,000 website references.

The Guinness World Records archivist Craig Glenday is a Mini enthusiast, fortunately, and he was only too pleased to delve into the stash of information about record attempts which never made the annual book. 'My first car was a Mini,' he told me, before fetching down files and checking out the firm's electronic archive. 'It was a beige automatic with virtually no brakes and no seatbelts (I had to pin a shoulder-bag strap across my chest when I drove to make it look as though I was strapped in). Beautiful thing it was. Unfortunately, I forgot to keep the water topped up, and the cap ended up melting into the radiator. Oh well ...'

The Mini contests are listed under 'Cramming' and they have quite a set of rules. Would-be record-breakers have to arrange for a doctor to be present and everyone taking part needs a medical certificate declaring them fit to be squashed briefly, agreeing that they have not been coerced and acknowledging that Guinness World Records is not responsible if anything goes wrong. The car has to be an original Mini Cooper, produced between 1961 and 1969 or 1996 and 2000, or a Cooper S, made between 1963 and 1971. They are slightly wider than the ordinary Mini, but not so that anyone inside with ridiculous numbers of other people would notice. 'No body parts may protrude,' says Rule Five and no one who is less than five feet or under eighteen years may take part. Every window must be closed, and while the doors can stay open until the last moment, they must then be fully shut by four volunteers stationed by each one, who have to step one full pace back from the car 'before quickly opening them again'.

Madness. But the record kept creeping up: nine originally, then slowly over forty years to fourteen, which is when the Reading Ladies rugby team decided to get involved. Striking a deal with Granada TV's *This Morning* programme, the women, some of whom are quite substantial, managed to cram a full rugby team of fifteen into a Cooper in September 1999. They were, and still are, a lively lot and through their social club of retired players, known as the Reading Winos, they had got to know the Guinness World Records people. Several took part in a throw and catch record attempt with assorted celebrities before the Mini-cramming notion was raised. Small car, large(ish) girls. It was ideal.

'We practised in a grotty old Mini at a factory unit in Reading belonging to the social secretary's Dad,' recalls Luan Read, a teacher and mother of two who still plays on the wing for the First XV. 'The suspension didn't like it, but we got the timing down to a T, and all our places inside sorted out. My bum was on the parcel shelf at the back. It wouldn't fit there now.' The record fell and their blood was up. Eight months later, they squeezed another two in on a special set created by Guinness in London. The hall rocked to the roars of rival supporters as another top women's team, the Wasps Ladies XV from West London, acted as challengers and pacemakers. While the Arsenal and England footballer Ian Wright supervised events, both teams broke the record. Sixteen Wasps, in their yellow and black strip, squashed into their Cooper alongside the Reading one on a glitzy stage. Both squads of women folded themselves carefully into a pre-arranged pattern, layered like large sardines up to the roof. 'Everyone has to make themselves little,' explained the Reading Ladies skipper, Clare Brooks, when asked about the team's strategy. 'Then you just get in there. Don't move, don't breathe, don't eat for a week beforehand, and you'll be fine.'

They were helped on the eating front, says Luan, by the fact that the event also included a woman with the world's record number of body piercings. 'That put us right off our dinner,' she laughed. 'It's hard to remember too much about the actual cramming because you can't see and you can't breathe.' There was a scary moment when the last door was about to be shut and yells went up of 'Watch her hair, it's in the door!' after the final player had wormed in backwards. Then the boot sprang open, revealing another team member somehow stashed between the petrol tank and the repair kit (no standard equipment could be moved under yet another rule). 'It had to be shut again and we all had to stay there for another five seconds,' says Luan. Nothing could stop them after that. In July 2000, they managed a staggering eighteen participants outside the National Indoor Arena in the Mini's home town of Birmingham.

Guinness now felt it necessary to warn excited would-be record-baggers that it would only accept attempts for three other vehicles: the Routemaster London bus (lower deck only, for safety reasons), the Smart car and the VW Beetle. The organisers also discouraged several attempts to think up new Mini-related challenges. But, as well as the largest parade, they agreed to accept the biggest mosaic made of the cars, which measured 53,280 square feet in the shape of the Mini logo at Verona in Italy. Two inventive engineers, Edd China and David Davenport, were also allowed the Fastest Furniture title, with a motorised sofa called The Casual Lofa which used a Mini engine and mechanics to reach 87mph.

The cramming title remained the Holy Grail, however,

and the hat-trick of records set by Reading's rugby-playing women was an irresistible gauntlet thrown down to dozens of other hopefuls. Attempt after attempt got close, but failed, until a group of Malaysian students at the International Technical College in Subang Jaya, near Kuala Lumpur, took things really seriously in July 2006. After several unsuccessful trawls, they managed to muster a team of entrants who each only just met Guinness height requirements and were notably skinny in build. The day of the college's annual charity fund-raising fair, monsoon rain poured down, but that only helped the students slither into their lime-green 1999 Mini Cooper. When nineteen-year-old Soong Vic Kie, who was especially sinuous, was squeezed into the boot, this time alongside another squashed-up young woman, there were twenty-one of them in the car. They stayed there for a full twenty seconds, well over the Guinness requirement, and then nonchalantly repeated the whole thing so that a TV crew could get them on film. 'We just thought of having a stunt to pull the crowd to our annual charity event but it turned out to be something much better,' said the students' leader Jasween Kaur Maan, modestly. 'It was uncomfortable in there, but everyone was too excited to complain.'

Will Reading strike back? 'It's a thought,' said Luan cautiously, settling down to work out how on earth you could fit yet another person into Issigonis' miraculous space. In essence, the rugby players' 2000 formation had one in the boot, three sat on the parcel shelf ('All with very short legs'), four on the back seat, two in the rear footwells, four on the front seats, two in the front wells, one under the windscreen and one along the dash. 'The Malaysians took our record because they were skinnier,' she continued. 'I guess we've got to find some players like that, so long as they're over five feet tall, and then work out whose bottom goes where.'

It is the stuff of literary epics. But it takes time for contemporary objects to make a great name in literature, and the Mini has only just started to find a niche. Many of Britain's current literary lions have owned one at some stage during their lives, usually a youthful period. The premier example is the white model run by Martin Amis when he was first making his name as a novelist. Known with good reason as the Ashtray, it has enjoyed a share of the publicity which has naturally attached itself to the successful son of a famous father (whose own novels featured young men such as Lucky Jim scooting about in the underpowered sports cars which were the 1950s version of Mini chic). The Ashtray is often mentioned in profiles of Amis junior and it took several bows in an exhibition at the National Portrait Gallery of photographs of him and his friends Ian McEwan and James Fenton, who have also gone on to publishing success. Neither Amis nor any of the now-celebrated passengers in the Ashtray have immortalised the car in prose or verse, but surely that time will come.

The world is awash with less distinguished examples of poetry about the Mini, written by owners about their particular car with a fervour which seems at odds with the fact that the car is seldom given an affectionate 'personal' name. There are exceptions; I have met members of the

Leeds Classic Mini Owners Club who have respectively a Mindy and a Minty, as well as Graham Bean's Merlin, but the habit is minimal compared to the Moggies, Millys, Mandys and the like bestowed on just about every surviving example of the Morris Minor. Professional poetry is approaching the Mini as a muse more cautiously, but there are examples. John Betjeman's 'Meditation on the A30' is notable for its title, quite apart from the actual verse, but it uses Issigonis' car to make a dark point. Written by an angry driver, frustrated both by a Mini blocking his way in heavy traffic and by his wife's loss of her looks and libido, the poem follows the two themes to their disastrous consequences:

'Why can't you step on it and shift her!
I can't go on crawling like this!
At breakfast she said that she wished I was dead –
Thank heavens we don't have to kiss ...

... You're barmy or plastered, I'll pass you, you bastard –
I will overtake you. I will!'
As he clenches his pipe, his moment is ripe
And the corner's accepting its kill.

The toll of the roads, far higher than deaths from violent crime, also exercised the writer J.G. Ballard, particularly in what he considered the pornographic context of lyrical advertising about the power, prestige and freedom of the car. He used a Mini in his deliberately shocking exhibition Crashed Cars, which was installed at the New Arts

Laboratory gallery in London in April 1970. The tableau was disgusting — a fatal, multiple-car crash treated as a public display complete with bloodstained victims — but that was the point. In addition to Ballard's counterpointing of the glamour and horror of cars and driving, the 'show' had lessons about the way that other drivers inevitably slow down to look at similar, real-life disasters on the road. Like the other two cars in the installation, the Mini was a very deliberate choice. It represented all the carefree, and often careless, fun associated with the car since Lord Snowdon's original patronage — that and the fragility, when it collided head-on with the likes of the other two cars, a baroque American Pontiac which represented florid wealth and power, and a staid Austin Cambridge A60, the type of so many soberly piloted saloons which get caught up in tragedy through their owners' complacency about the risk of other, wilder drivers' mistakes.

The opening night of the exhibition realised all Ballard's fears — or anticipations — as guests became drunk and laughed and flirted within touching distance of the staged carnage. Ever the provocateur, the author arranged for a topless woman to wander around the proceedings with a camcorder, interviewing guests about their increasingly incoherent opinions of the event, which were then broadcast on CCTV. As the drink took effect, wine was poured over the cars, broken window glass kicked around, and, according to Ballard, the topless interviewer was nearly raped in the Pontiac's back seat. Later visitors also seemed infected by similar impulses, and the cars were vandalised, covered in graffiti and urinated in, to an extent that astonished even staff at the Motor Crash Repairs company in Hackney which had hired them to Ballard and his colleagues. All the exhibition cars were genuine crash wrecks which the firm had been planning to repair. The Mini, according to the author in his 'fictionalised autobiography' *The Kindness of Women*, had rolled down a motorway embankment after a crash and still had grass growing in its windowsills.

Ballard was on target in his choice of the little car as an innocent-looking fun motor which could suddenly become a death trap. There are other dark sides to its history. Myra Hindley drove one, a pale blue saloon with the registration OEK 749B which she used when enticing the child victims of the Moors Murders to the house she shared with Ian Brady. Stephen Waldorf, an innocent young film editor notoriously mistaken for an escaped criminal, was shot by police at the wheel of his yellow Mini in a traffic jam on Knightsbridge in 1983. Five shots struck him at close range and another nine were fired at the car, but remarkably, he survived. Then Ballard's lasting fascination with the car and death had reached a grim apogee with the most famous fatal accident of the late twentieth century: and again it was a Mini involved. Princess Diana died in the back seat of a Mercedes Benz, but the chauffeur Henri Paul used a Mini as his private car. Two days after the tragedy, it was found in an underground car park, and much photographed; its mild, familiar 'face' above the registration 766 KZT 75 forming a striking contrast for media picture editors with the carnage in the Place de L'Alma underpass.

Ballard's preoccupations continue to resonate; in August 2008 a street-art festival in London chose the classically dystopian setting of the Leake Street pedestrian underpass at Waterloo for an exhibition of burnt out cars, boldly streaked with graffiti. Some had conventional 'tags' sprayed on them, others were more delicately painted with stencilled patterns under the curatorship of the best-known street artist of the day, the anonymous Banksy. The Mini involved, an old 1980s model resting on its wheel-hubs with the tyres burned off, stood out because of its vivid colours, which dripped off it in wavering stripes like a barcode gone dreadfully wrong.

Sometimes bright young Mini owners got away with potentially disastrous behaviour on the road. The singer Will Young admits to a teenage episode when he drunkenly drove his Mini the wrong way up a one-way street in Oxford and crashed into a police car. The officers' patience was tried further by the fact that the car's doors, never a perfect fit, jammed completely and Young couldn't obey their instruction to get out. He ended up handcuffed in court where he was banned for eighteen months; an episode which determined him never to drink-drive again.

No one has ever solved the cause of the most notorious Mini crash, which had no happy endings but fitted to a T Jim Ballard's theories about celebrities and death on the roads. Early in the morning of 16 September 1977, Marc Bolan of the legendary rock combo T. Rex slipped merrily into the passenger seat of a purple Austin Mini 1275GT, the high-powered successor to the Cooper, after dinner with his American partner Gloria Jones, back-up singer and mother of their two-year-old son Rolan. Bolan was fascinated by cars, often bringing them into his songwriting lyrics, but had never learned to drive. So it was Gloria who was at the wheel when the Mini left the road just after a hump-backed bridge on the edge of Barnes Common in London. It slewed sideways through a fence and smashed into a sycamore, Bolan's side taking the full impact, which flung him into the back of the car, killing him instantly. There were no seat-belts, let alone airbags or steel protective frames, and Gloria was also knocked unconscious and badly injured.

Bolan's career had been on the slide. Unable to keep reinventing himself, as his friend and contemporary David Bowie had, he finished up as host of a children's TV show. But the manner of his death brought all the old glamour back to life. Bowie was joined by Elton John, Rod Stewart and many other stars at the funeral in Golders Green crematorium and in due course the T. Rex Appreciation Society bought the sycamore and was given a perpetual lease on the rest of the crash site, which members have since maintained as a wild garden. In 2002 Rolan Bolan launched his own singing career by unveiling a bronze bust of his father there and five years later the English Tourist Board gave the ultimate Ballardian seal to the whole performance. Their booklet *England Rocks* included it among essential sights for swingers, with the official title of Marc Bolan's Rock Shrine. The Mini, however, registration number FOX 661L, has been scrapped.

After this grim episode, it is a relief to turn to the pages of the Molly Mini series which Alison Orchard Hammill, a grandmother living in Devon, began in response to requests from her grandsons. There are no crashes here, but a mildly adventurous life based in Exmouth where Molly the Mini and her friend Minnie enter surprise car shows, help with breakdowns and generally potter around. Mrs Hammill has seen life – brought up in Sierra Leone, Ghana and Zambia, she worked as a nurse, dental assistant, bookkeeper and caretaker before lighting off for Zimbabwe from London overland in a converted 1956 Bedford ambulance. Aimed at four- to eight-year-olds, Molly Mini is branded as being 'educational and covering courtesy, manners and being helpful to others', but its publishers would also please Jim Ballard. Quite apart from the books, your children or grandchildren can pester you for such items as a Molly Mini babygro and hat combo, a pair of scratch mittens or – very up to date – a fiftieth-anniversary-of-the-Mini popover bib.

The new MINI is meanwhile developing a cultural role, appropriate for Britain's changing social mores, as a 'gay car', alongside its different reputations as a chickmobile and a classy little two-fingers to outdated Mums who insist on lumbering about in pretend jeeps. Started by French enthusiasts in the Club Auto Rainbow in 2004, the Gay Car of the Year competition was rapidly copied in Britain and the MINI was well up there, although the Smart car won the first poll of members in 2006 by the gay website Outuk.com. The MINI came a respectable fifth, both for its looks, and, as Mike Gray of Outuk said, echoing the comments fifty years before from Peter Sellers and Lord Snowdon, 'A large number of gays are urban and these cars are practical for city living.' The car's success was appropriate, too, because of a 'MINI Adventure' which was not immortalised in BMW's series of nifty TV adverts on that theme. Soon after the new car's launch, MINI had the chance to take part in the Gay Pride Mardi Gras festival in London and couldn't resist a bit of cheek, because the main car sponsor of the event was Ford. There in the colourful procession was an 'S&M MINI' kitted out in black leather and with punitive equipment on board.

Both old and new versions of the car have seen limited 'art editions' as marketing ploys, using celebrities to suggest decorations for distinctive livery. Mary Quant produced a black-and-white car in 1987, with the Cooper stripe motif repeated in a zebra pattern on the seat upholstery. Paul Smith, the designer, went for stripes like Quant but many more of them in a vivid range of colours, sideways along the body: a carcode barcode. The model Kate Moss, involved to recall the tradition of Jean Shrimpton and her colleagues in the Mini's Swinging Sixties heyday, came up with a delicate spider's web pattern for the car's fiftieth-birthday celebrations in 1999. It went down well, although the success did not protect her from paparazzi photographers who filmed her taking ten minutes to inch her own, white Mini into a tight-fit London parking bay. The same year, Damien Hirst painted a Mini with his trademark coloured spots to be auctioned for charity at an event marking the thirtieth anniversary of the Serpentine Gallery in London's Hyde Park. There was an interesting sequel. The 'London Spot Mini' was bought by Charles Saatchi and played a part in a feud between the two men which broke out several years later. When the Mini was given a central position at the entrance to the Saatchi Gallery in 2003, frozen in mid-career down the faux-baroque stairway of the former Greater London Council HQ in an echo of the Coopers' exploits in *The Italian Job*, Hirst exploded. An artist much scorned by traditionalist critics for producing 'non art', he took that view himself of the Mini, declaring that it was never intended to be more than a fun charity fundraiser. Shortly afterwards, he bought back a third of his work in Saatchi's collection.

What would Hirst and Saatchi have made of the most recent form of Mini art: the extraordinary 'dust paintings' of Scott Wade, an American artist who lives on the edge of Austin, the state capital of Texas? He has a modern MINI, which is earning a cool but comfy and safe reputation in the States in a way which its predecessor never managed, and he lives at the end of an unmade dirt road. The combination has led to Wade's own transitory but remarkable take on artists' age-old experimentation with images and ways of recording them.

As he thrashed the car – inevitably a Cooper – up and down Roadrunner Road, the bumpy track of broken limestone which leads to his home in San Marcos, Wade noticed how a thick film of dust built up on the wide back window of the car. One day, before going in to have supper with his wife Robin and their cat Squeek, he traced a fingernail line across the patina. Then another. And another. The result has been a series of complex pictures, delicate not only in the original composition, which is rather like an etcher's work on wax, but in the way that Wade follows their change and eventual disintegration because of the weather. Early morning dew on the window, he records, creates one particular kind of slightly blurry, French Impressionist patina. Light rainfall makes another. Wade has also subjected his studies of the 'Mona Lisa', Van Gogh's 'Starry Night' and a take on C.M. Coolidge's sentimental poker dogs' picture 'A Friend in Need', to applications of almond oil, tree sap and the ministrations of Squeek.

The cat's contribution came one morning after Wade had etched a portrait of Einstein on to his back window. 'Squeek wanted to express himself on Albert's forehead,' explained the artist, who has thick tousled hair, a beard and a quizzical look. 'I had walked out one morning to finish this piece, and found Squeek had beat me to it.' In other words, sat on the roof of the car and weed down the back. 'Now, if a cat can do it, what are you waiting for? Dust art is for everyone.'

Wade has used all his fingers, a range of paint brushes and bits of old popsicles, or what in Britain would be called lolly sticks, to etch his designs. None of them last on the window, but all are immortalised – and internetted – thanks to digital photography and the computer. One picture even played a small part in US politics. It showed a portrait of Kinky Friedman, the poet, singer and election hopeful in the race to be Texas governor in 2006, along with a slogan urging other drivers to vote for him. The dust picture made it to Kinky's website, although it didn't work the magic for him. He managed just over 12 per cent of the vote.

If this obsessive attitude appeals to you, it may be time to invest in the niche market of 'Mini music', which is growing vigorously. The car has played bit parts in songs and on record sleeves since 1959, but it comes into its own with ringtones. There's the relatively conventional option, such as Madonna singing in her 2003 number 'American Life': 'I drive my Mini Cooper/And I'm feeling super-dooper.' But aficionados of specialist tones want *car* noise, and it's all here. The Mini Cooper alone offers eleven seconds of driving, slowing and stopping, a bumper thirty-eight seconds of starting, driving, slowing and stopping and, for the really devoted connoisseur, a delicate six seconds of the key being inserted into the ignition, withdrawn and then reinserted. To the layman, it sounds like a series of small clicks which might suggest that something has gone wrong with the phone. But these ringtones are not for the layman. They cover the demands of those who like their Minis big and beastly, modest and quiet, roofless, four-wheel-drive, cut in half, trebled in length or just plain weird. Over fifty years, the car has been all those, and much more.

## Chapter Nine
# The Long, the Short and the Tall

*'We will never change the shape.'*
*Alec Issigonis' handwritten note in his copy of*
The Mini Story

 WHAT IS THE CHIEF DISTINCTION of the Mini?
Easy. It is small. But not small enough for
everyone, as you discover when you meet
Holly Brown-Horsley, keeper of the Mini
Shorty Register. You need to look quickly to
catch a glimpse of her and her car, a tiny white bug with pink
painted flowers scattered all over it. A standard Mini is 120
inches long. Holly's diced and re-assembled mini-Mini is 76
inches. When she parks, people stop and ask her, 'Is that a
real car?' Indeed, when she first saw one, she wondered: 'Is
it just too tiny and silly?' Her next thought was: 'I *want*
that car.'

She had to wait for eight years after that first sighting,
building up her career as a graphic artist in the meanwhile.
The pink flowers on her Shorty are an example of her work,
part of the portfolio she takes to clients. Then she saw
another hacked-down Mini advertised, did the deal and took
to the road, although only after an official from the Driving

and Vehicle Licensing Authority had paid her a home visit. It was probably partly curiosity, but he said that he had to check that this oddity was roadworthy. Given the go-ahead, she started shopping by Shorty, then commuting to work and finally heading further afield. Her home and office are in Huntingdonshire, but the car has ranged much more widely than that. While her husband Michael flicked through a series of pictures of the car on his mobile phone, Holly listed some of her epic journeys. 'Cambridge is a regular, then there's London, oh, and Brighton. I've done 70mph comfortably, although I'd say as a rule that when you're in a Shorty, you drive carefully.'

The usual feeling of vulnerability in a Mini on a motorway, or anywhere near large lorries, is redoubled when you are in not much more than half a car. Holly and Michael draw reassurance from being squeezed into the Shorty together, and from the universal fondness they encounter on the roads. 'It wouldn't be a car for a wallflower,' she says. 'When you're out driving it's just honk, honk, honk and waves and smiles all the time.'

Holly came from a Mini home; her mother and father had one and she caught their enthusiasm early. She and Mike had a Mini-themed wedding and their house overflows with models, jewellery, stuffed toys and garden furniture based on the car. One display has pink model Minis, from a sort of jumbo Dinky version to Matchbox size; corner shelves have Minis coming out of racetrack dioramas and there's a sinister black two-centimetre model made of Whitby jet. Holly's Mini bracelet includes a tiny Traveller, a couple of saloons and of course a Shorty, but no van. She couldn't find one the right size, so had to settle for a larger version on a pendant. The garden is meanwhile prowled by radio-controlled Minis, including another Shorty in the same livery as her real one. There's also a stonking marriage between a one-twelfth scale model Mini and one of those outsize model jeeps with tractor wheels which can clamber over flowerbeds and rockeries.

Holly and Mike belong to the Huntingdon Area Mini Owners Club, and her website for the Shorty Register (www.forum.hollysminis.co.uk/index.php) keeps growing. Its pages show how to make a Shorty in four simple steps: essentially, cut off the front and rear of an ordinary Mini, remove the middle bit – length to taste – and then fit them carefully together again. 'The smallest ones I've seen are "Dutchends", where the car finishes at the end of the front window, with the rear angled steeply down from there,' she said. Overall length in her experience is from 103 inches down to 76, although there are almost certainly shorter Shorties out there, not yet on her register.

Shorty fans have started their own rally at Stanford Hall in Leicestershire – a modest affair like the car, with six or seven turning up last year, but, as with the register and website, interest is growing. Another of Mike's phone pictures shows four rally cars lined up in the hall's grounds, including a shortened Mini Cooper with not much boot but a proper battery of four extra lights mounted on its radiator grille. There's a mass of information on the website to help Shorty owners download and exchange pictures of their tiny beasts, although the technical page currently ends abruptly: 'To be completed ... *Top Gear* is on.'

Buying a working Mini Shorty can set you back £4,500 – the price asked online for one in 2007 by an owner who didn't attempt to disguise the basic nature of pint-sized motoring. His was a convertible with no doors – 'so you have to climb in' – and it had never been out in the rain. But the car, originally made in 1967, was tax-exempt and its parts had been carefully separated and then rejoined in a full restoration after he bought it on eBay. But prices vary hugely. A similar tiny, roofless version went on sale in Johannesburg in March 2009 for 1,800 rand, only £1,360. Jet black with flame decals along its sides and scarlet seats, it is in daily use. But South Africa is hot and sunny.

From the very short to the very long: after all Sir Alec Issigonis had done to keep his new baby within ten feet from bonnet to boot, a cult developed to see how big and/or beastly it could be made. And, for a car mechanic called Lindsay Taylor-Haynes and his mates in the local pub, how far it could be s-t-r-e-t-c-h-e-d. The group of them worked in a business which picked up on the 1990s fashion for converting ordinary cars into limousines for weddings, teens going to school proms and other such events, a trend copied as ever from the United States. 'Has anyone ever stretched a Mini?' Lindsay wondered over his pint. They checked and found several, but none of them up to the standard they felt the little classic deserved. Lindsay's father was a structural engineer and he looked into the stresses and loadings involved. It would work, he decided, but there would have to be a precisely calculated main frame and a fair amount of new steel. Lindsay was up for that, and so began some 4000 hours of assembly work, stopping and starting as funds came and went, and using a 1969 Mini Cooper, supplemented by two other Minis and the extra metal recommended by Taylor-Haynes senior.

The result is a 35ft super-Mini with a 1430cc engine, dual braking systems and the usual glitz of a limo inside – TV screen, cocktail bar and table, fluted champagne glasses to hand. It was a regular feature at Mini enthusiasts' gatherings in the 1990s and the scene of a romantic moment in 1996, when Lindsay and his partner entered it for that year's Italian Job Rally. En route to Turin they got engaged, and in due course the car took Sharon to church for their wedding and left with both of them on honeymoon. It later ferried Kevin Spacey round London for his 39th birthday before finally heading off to the original land of the limo. Another enthusiast, Harry Bullens, saw it at the Birmingham Classic Car Show in 2002 with a For Sale sign in the window and was instantly on the phone to Jan Harde, a friend in Los Angeles who had pined for a Mini limo for years. When last heard of, it had been fitted with a DVD system, ice boxes and burr walnut armrests and gearstick knob, although much of this detail is often hidden under the owner's collection of Teddy bears. Lindsay's mechanics, which included bits of a Saab and other cannibal parts, have been adjusted a little too, to avoid the car overheating in its new and warmer home.

Thirty-five foot is a shorty, however, compared to some other bizarrely enlarged Minis, notably a bilious yellow one originally concocted by a British enthusiast, John Hodge. Using a Metro engine and disc brakes, he first produced a thin, squeezed saloon, fairly standard by the lights of this sub-culture, but then felt that it wasn't anything like long enough. So he chopped a Riley Elf in half and added the bits to the front and back of his yellow slug. The final length from eyelid headlamps to jaunty rear fins was 50ft, five times the length of Issigonis' original passenger cabin. Talk about spinning in the grave. The car creaked majestically around Britain for a while before going to a buyer in the Bahamas and then to Jeff Drago in Washington state, who replaced the Elf additions with a conventional 'round nose' front and standard rear, losing a little length to restore the classic look, sort of.

At the time of writing in June 2009, one of these beasts was up for sale in Malton, North Yorkshire, an hour's drive from my home in Leeds. But I didn't go to have a look, because I cannot get my head round the notion of enlarging a car whose whole purpose was to be small. Others seem to feel the same; after nearly two months on eBay with a reserve price of £4000, the car had yet to attract a bid. That was despite the fact that it was a stretch convertible, adding to its unreal air, and a car with a bit of a history: it ferried the Spice Girls to the Brit Awards in London in 1998. It was shiny black then and covered with sequins, most of which are still hanging on, but, as the seller honestly admitted, 'the colour is now black with a heavy metal flake – it does show some signs of being a more greeny colour. The front seats are well worn and the signatures on the bootlid (of Geri,

Posh & Co) are not genuine.' Still, it had four new tyres, a nearly new hood and an MoT which only expired in July.

A man who would certainly have ideas for it is Tony 'Waspy' Anchors of Didcot, a self-confessed 'bodgerologist' who has turned Mini successively into a double-decker sight-seeing bus, with room for six on the open-top upper deck, a mobile bar with space for eight drinkers, and a working paddle steamer. This ended up at the bottom of an orna-mental lake at Birmingham's National Exhibition Centre, but Waspy was not discouraged. His other creations have included a Noddy Mini, another carrying its own garden in bloom and a version with slats on the roof which folded down to make a portable garage.

Minis have been chopped and changed since their earliest days, not only by individualistic owners but by the car's official manufacturers. Issigonis said famously that his con-cept would never alter, as per his note in his copy of Laurence Pomeroy's *The Mini Story* – but it soon did, some-times massively. Pomeroy himself includes a photograph of one of the earliest but vastest oddities, an eight-wheel trailer-truck created by Thornewell Meats to deliver their pies. There was a trial all-electric Mini as early as 1966 and Issigonis experimented with a version powered by steam. More commonly, and so far as BMC's official derivatives were concerned, the changes were much smaller, but in the Lilliput context of the Mini, the smallest change is significant.

The first variant became one of the most famous, not so much for its shape as for its price. If the original cars were a bargain then the Minivan was an absolute steal. It appeared in May 1960, eight months after the marque's launch, and in the sluggish early market for the car its success had a significant impact on sales. It was slightly larger, the wheels three inches further apart and the length up by ten inches to ten feet ten inches, but it was a *lot* cheaper. Free of purchase tax, on the grounds that a van had business use – in reviving, post-war Britain that deserved a fiscal break – it undercut the saloon by £146 19s 2d and cost only £360. This was a remarkable bargain in a market where the cheapest new car of any sort was the increasingly venerable Ford Popular, at £494 2s 6d including tax. The Minivan was also a practical vehicle for those buyers – a definite minority – who genuinely wanted one for business use. Thanks to the transverse engine in its snug bonnet, the rear platform was two inches longer than the one in the rival A35, even though that van overall was eight inches longer.

The Minivan's users soon included the AA and many police forces, adding to an air of reliability which sales brochures played up. The concept that 'small is beautiful' had yet to come into play – E.F. Schumacher's famous book was not published until 1973 – and BMC was more concerned to emphasise that the Mini's commercial version was sturdy. Pictures of an AA patrolman and a Panda car being admired by a gaggle of children were used in marketing, along with the slogan: 'Strength and Stamina – although small in size the Mini lacks nothing in either.' Real-life policing also provided helpful publicity, for example when the brilliant but wayward Manchester United foot-baller George Best was escorted from the city's magistrates' courts in a very smart staff Mini. He had just been given a conditional discharge for drunkenly assaulting a young woman in a nightclub; not the last time that he, drink, the police and one of the cars were to form a headline-grabbing combination. The *Daily Mail* protested about over-generous use of official Minis on another occasion, when a decoy panda was parked outside a London court where the foot-baller was acquitted of another bit of wild behaviour, while Best was smuggled out at the back in a Minivan.

The bobby in the front passenger seat on the Manchester occasion looked extremely uncomfortable, not surprisingly because he was wearing his beat officer's helmet, which forces soon learned was not advisable in their minimalist new cars. 'We always used our peaked traffic-officer caps,' recalled Danny Ewington, whose voice filled with nostalgic yearning as he told me about his heyday roaring along Victoria Avenue East – 'the widest, fastest road in Manchester' – chasing villains who regularly topped 100mph. 'It's a thirty limit now; rather a shame,' he said, as we swapped tales of forces who used the Cooper's pop-pop-bang blowback, when you crash down the gears, outside the homes of known criminals before breakfast, when they were reckoned to be sleeping-in after a night of burgling.

Manchester's traffic officers thought that all their birthdays had come at once when the city's force, since merged into Greater Manchester Police, ordered a fleet of Mini Cooper 1250Ss in 1968. 'I can still remember my registration plate –

how sad am I?' laughed Ewington, who keeps paintings of all his police cars hanging on the walls at home near Oldham. 'The wife's work,' he explained. Christine Ewington, a talented amateur artist, enjoyed painting JNB 11F. 'A brilliant little car,' sighed Danny, although it wasn't completely brilliant when he first started driving it. The Coopers were supposed to do 82mph in third gear, but Danny's was having trouble getting much over 70. He asked the section's head, a traditionally dour Mancunian, if it could be stripped down and checked.

'Ewington,' said the Chief Inspector. 'They can do it but if there's nothing wrong, you're back on division' – i.e. foot patrol. It was a nervous couple of days but Danny's hunch was right. Somehow, on the assembly line at Longbridge, the Mini had been fitted with a Morris 1300 engine by mistake, and so wasn't a Cooper at all. 'There was another time when I couldn't get over 72mph in third,' he adds, 'but that was because I had a punctured front tyre.'

The Coopers – which Liverpool police also ordered, along with Southend-on-Sea which had a squadron of gleaming white ones – were the sharp end of the police Mini-world. Many more forces went for straightforward 850cc models for community work, when panda cars controversially replaced the bobby on the beat. They were deliberately cosy, according to John Endicott at Kent police forces' museum, although the transport section there went for Hillman Imps instead. Colleagues of John remember the little cars being lined up in parades, in an attempt to win over the sceptical public as well as give a modest show of strength. It was the same in Manchester, said Ewington, where the Coopers had forty standard Mini panda counterparts. They went down well, and he remembered affectionate looks when he was sent to escort 500-tonne transformers from the Ferranti works on their way to Africa. These were so heavy that special trailers originally designed to carry complete hovercraft had to be brought in, to distribute a load which, concentrated, would have damaged the road. Ahead of them, in another of his proudest moments, tootled PC Ewington in his little car.

Police Minis had few disadvantages, he reckoned, although the George Best photograph illustrated one of them: 'There are inherent difficulties in getting a prisoner into the back of a Mini Cooper S.' Officers making an arrest had to radio for the nearest of the force's prison vans which patrolled in areas where the Minis were making forays, like a fishing fleet's mother ship. Duncan Brodie, who runs Manchester's police museum, where Danny leads tours, mused: 'It's interesting that forces went for the country's smallest car at a time when police officers had to be six feet tall.' But it worked. Danny never felt squashed in his Cooper, and he is six feet two inches.

Other advertisements for the Mini's commercial uses were less dramatic: artists were hired by BMC to portray a gently coloured-in Ladybird Books world, in which reliable tradesmen toured the suburbs, capably mending things. A typical example has one car belonging to Mr C. Plumber the builder, who is up a ladder dealing with roof tiles, admired by a smiling young housewife with a baby on her arm. In the foreground, Mr A. Baker is unloading fresh bread from his Minivan, to bring a smile to someone else's face.

No advertisements were needed, however, for the van to attract the likes of Christine Perry, the schoolgirl whose science teacher in Longbridge got so excited about the transverse engine in 1959. It wasn't long before her boyfriend got hold of one, cut windows in the side panels and invited their local posse for drives. A gang of six of them squeezed into the back, head to tail like sardines, with another two in the driver and passenger seat upfront. Everyone was doing it. Martin and Mary Iles, now in their fifties and dealers in motorbikes at Portishead, have been through half a dozen Minis, but the one they remember most fondly was a van. 'We had a green one, didn't we – our very first car,' mused Martin when the three of us met at a nostalgic Sixties exhibition in York. Then he was off recalling his own window-cutting exploits and fixing some sort of passenger comfort in the back. Not always for everyone. 'I remember going down to Torquay in a friend's Minivan. He met a girl there and they got together. That's why I ended up sleeping on the roof.' Thanks to such a range of uses, from the police and Mr A. Baker to Martin's friend, the range proved lastingly popular, holding its place as Britain's best-selling small van until the late 1970s, when it was still selling more than 10,000 a year. It was renamed the Mini 95 in 1978, to highlight its gross weight of 0.95 tonnes, and production only stopped in 1982, when more modern and sophisticated replacements finally overtook it in the market's league table. By then, a total of 521,494 had been made.

The main car, the Mark I as the original Austin Se7en and Morris Mini-Minor were classified, lasted until 1967, with a steady series of variants following the van. First, and also exempt from purchase tax, came the Mini Pickup in 1961, a van topless apart from its cab and with added utility features which enhanced its appeal. The austerity which initially discouraged Mini buyers looking for a new family saloon was a positive incentive for the practical types who formed most of the pickup's buyers. The standard chrome radiator grille, for example, was replaced with simple stamped-metal slots which sent air flowing into the engine space. You could have a heater, but only as an extra. It was a little truck for little businesses, and a total of 58,179 were sold.

The car had now settled into a sequence successfully pioneered by the Morris Minor, whose own van and pickup versions were still selling well. But they had been comfortably beaten in popularity by the wood-framed Morris Minor Traveller – the 'woodie' estate car which prompted Barry Humphries as Dame Edna Everage to note, on a TV tour of Stratford upon Avon, that 'even the cars here are half-timbered'. Naturally the Mini deserved to have one of those as well. It duly appeared in 1961, keeping up the high standard of Austin/Morris confusion by using two names, the Traveller or the Countryman, but both had the same side-opening 'barn doors' at the back and, in their luxury versions, the woodie timber glued on. As with the Traveller, this soon became a source of stories about carrying your own mushroom farm and warning the children against splinters as the ash deteriorated. The combined sales of the two models fell way behind the van's, an interesting difference from the Morris Minor market, where the van never became seen as super-cool, but they were still respectable. When they were replaced in 1969 by British Leyland's new concept, the Mini Clubman, the Traveller had topped 99,000 and the Countryman 108,000.

The car which I fantasised about owning more than any other, as a teenager, appeared in 1965: the Mini-Moke, designed originally for military use but never high enough off the ground for the forces to get any practical use out of it. Although it was light enough for a couple of burly soldiers to lift off any hummock or boulder, should it become grounded, the fatal deterrent for the Ministry of Defence was that in rough conditions troops would end up humping their Mokes around almost all the time. It was a shame, because the pared-down little jeep had the closest ancestry of all the Minis to Issigonis' wartime creations. When saloon-car development was banned by the government, he was diverted to making a range of peculiar experimental military vehicles, notably the Nuffield Guppy, a sort of amphibious, powered wheelbarrow for ferrying supplies, which emerges from swamps in archive photographs resembling a mixture between a Moke and a large newt. Designing them was enjoyably stimulating because convention was pushed aside. One of Issigonis' colleagues Sid Goble, who became chief stylist at Morris, had a wonderful time on secondment to the 79th armoured division designing a range of strange flail-wielding and bridge-laying tanks which became collectively known as

'Hobart's Funnies' after the armoured vehicle specialist Percy Hobart who supervised the secret scheme. But like Issigonis' lightweight racing cars, these experiments allowed serious and very early trials of systems such as torsion-bar independent front-wheel suspension and even transverse engines. In the Moke they came to fruition and commercial sale.

The jeeplet was launched in January 1963, when its design team were among very few people in Britain who celebrated that year's icy weather. Abundant snow and slush allowed the launch ceremony to show off the Moke's four-wheel-drive traction at parts of Longbridge which resembled ski slopes and an ice rink. It was perhaps appropriate, however, that the celebratory party included the comedian Norman Wisdom, as the Moke was to lead a very different life from the rugged challenges its marketing implied. Rejected by the military, and indeed by ski resorts, which wanted much larger tractors and caterpillar vehicles, it became another 'accessory' Mini for the well-off and well-known – the beach and holiday version of the Mini de Villes and their fancy counterparts commissioned by celebrities for town use. It was rapidly advertised not in the company of menacing soldiers, but with two very unmilitary-looking young women on board, curled up respectively on the bonnet and passenger seat against a background of sun umbrellas and yachts. There was no smarter accessory on the upmarket beach.

As a result, some 50,000 models were made of this impractical but extremely enjoyable fun-car, with a further hand to its cult status coming from a star role in *The Prisoner*, the 1967 TV series set in Portmeirion and starring Patrick McGoohan which still retains a devoted following. The sinister, sealed community in which the drama is set used a white-painted Moke with a fringed surrey canopy on top, one of twenty conversions produced by Crayford Engineering of Westerham, Kent, which had pioneered £150 convertible packages for Minis in 1963. The other nineteen went abroad to join the Beach Mini in servicing posh hotels. The little jeep, whose name is a now largely forgotten slang word for a donkey, ceased production in Britain the following year but was made in Australia until 1982 and production continued in Portugal for another eleven years, after an Italian firm bought the rights from British Leyland to carry the line on. Ground clearance problems did not deter an order from the police in the former Portuguese colony of Macau, which has its share of the two-in-one gradients singled out in BMC advertising as no problem for the sturdy little four-wheel drive. Enthusiasts are concentrated in Australia these days, largely for climate reasons, and they managed to get 161 of the cars to a Moke Muster in 2006 and even more in the birthday year – Mini 50, Moke 45 – of 2009, at a Mokefest in Wagga Wagga.

The celebrity customising of Minis and the freelance industry in souping-up kits meanwhile prompted a quick response from BMC. Issigonis never much cared for either of them, but the Riley Elf and Wolseley Hornet were designed as upmarket versions of the standard model, not merely with a little more comfort internally but a supposedly classier overall look. Upright radiators, small boots and rear fins were the main external difference, along with larger bumpers and extra chrome. Inside, a much wider dashboard made of wood veneer replaced the idiosyncratically miniaturist panel of the original Mini, which was useful if sacrilege to those of an austere, Issigonis mind.

Both cars took their names from small creatures but ones with a sporty past; the first Wolseley Hornet was a 1930s sports car and the Elf had deliberate echoes of Riley's Sprite and Imp, which were rivals of the original Hornets at track races. As the Mini developed its Cooper versions, both were also upgraded, increasing their engine capacity from 848cc to 998cc in 1963. Other heresies added as the marques progressed were wind-up windows and concealed door hinges. Sales were very similar: 28,455 Hornets and 30,912 Elfs.

The Mark II upgrading of the whole Mini range in 1967 brought major and unwelcome changes in the car's appearance, with the fitting of a wider radiator grille with headlights inset on either side. The result gave less of the innocent but knowing look of the original which had struck Peter Ustinov on his first encounter with the car. In his address at Issigonis' funeral in December 1988 he expanded on this: 'The Mini had a character which is exactly like his. It has a look with its headlights of innocence but at the same time of extreme sophistication and of a slight inability to grow up, a sort of Peter Pan quality.'

The Mark II was a blow to the iconic Mini style, but

Longbridge stuck with it. Within two years, the new look was incorporated in the Clubman upgrade, designed by the stylist, perhaps better called clumsyist, Roy Haynes for the car's new producers British Leyland. This alteration also added boxiness, a characteristic of Haynes' previous work for Ford, and thereby lost more of the childlike softness of Issigonis' gently rounded original lines. The front in particular was different, replacing the Mini's round nose with a squared-off section, which used the same sidelight and indicator units as the new but much less popular Austin Maxi. It was optimistically advertised by film clips of young women with psychedelic patterns moving across their mid-riffs while disco lights changed colours in the background. The message was groovy, clubby, young and funsterish, all qualities which the original Mini had transmitted much more subtly, without stating the obvious.

The Clubman class included Sir Donald Stokes' alternative to the Mini Cooper, following his decision that the £2 royalty paid to John Cooper on each car was a waste of money. The 1275GT Mini was a sophisticated car but never remotely a match for the Cooper, slowed by inferior engine tuning and a less aerodynamic shape which made anything more than 90mph a struggle. On ordinary roads, this mattered less than on the racetrack or rally circuit, and the car's cheaper insurance won it a reasonable market, particularly in the absence of the Cooper, which only continued in production under licence for a year or so in Italy and, until 1972, in Australia, where a slightly less powerful variant of the Cooper engine and disc brakes were concealed in a Clubman body and sold as the Clubman GT. Production of the round-nosed original Mini meanwhile soldiered on and eventually outlasted the Clubmans, which ceased production in 1980. By then 275,583 of the type's saloon, 197,606 Clubman Estates and 110,673 1275GTs had been made.

The variants grew and grew, and when in 1999 the Motor Heritage Centre threw a fortieth-birthday bash for the car at Silverstone grand prix circuit, they counted 133 different official models. The alterations were not always on the outside; cars which looked similar to the layman could have very different systems under the bonnet, such as those made between 1964 and 1971, when the hydrolastic suspension system which Alex Moulton had studied and experimented with for years was introduced. The ride was softer but the handling less precise and the return to rubber cones was generally welcomed. Much more dramatic mechanical changes were planned for a new mini-Mini, designed by Issigonis as a shorter but more powerful replacement for the car, which reached the stage of an experimental model called 9X in 1970. But British Leyland was by then wracked with the internal squabbles which became its hallmark and the project was abandoned.

The big carmaker's failure of nerve was not reflected in the thriving conversion market, which was the happy home of less exalted contempories of Issigonis, innovators and dreamers who were bubbling with their own plans for taking the car forward. From the Gnat and the Gecko to the Minnow and the Minette, there were another 130 versions of the car produced during its lifetime, chopped-down, souped-up and in the case of the Minissima, which BL briefly considered producing as an urban predecessor of the Smart car in 1973, with only a single entrance via a door at the rear. One of the most successful was the Scamp, a kit car based for nearly twenty years on the Mini frame, although since a takeover in 1989 the makers have gone for bigger versions using Daihatsu and Suzuki chassis. The car started life with the death of the Moke, when a number of enthusiasts decided that the strange but appealing little jeep should continue in other, and if possible more practical forms. Most efforts fell by the wayside but Robert Mandry, working in the Surrey village of Ottershaw, persisted and found a market for some 200 cars a year. Initially angular and later boxy, Scamps had no pretensions to Mini stylishness but were built to last. Their bodyframe used high quality tubular steel and aluminium to avoid the Mini's tendency to rust. They were cheerfully Moke-like and determinedly all-purpose; Scamp owners carted things about in them or took them off road and had fun. The RTV version, for particularly rough terrain, could manage extraordinary manoeuvres with suspension and steering which allowed the front wheels to twist at impossible-looking angles to extricate the car from ditches or tackle steep, broken ground. Mounted on vast wheels like a child's Tonka toy, it looked as butchly different from its little parent as could possibly be.

Mandry's inventiveness was matched by Peter Pellandine, who adapted his name just slightly for the Pellandini adaption of the Mini, a racing coupé with astonishing acceleration and gull wings. Pellandine was another clever man-in-a-garage, like Bill Cull of the Rzeppa continuous velocity joint, the type that gave the post-war British car industry much of its flair. He set up a business in 1955, in a lock-up next to the Robin Hood pub in Epping Forest, making curving, stylish body shells out of fibreglass for sports-car enthusiasts to fit to old Austin 7 frames or small Fords. In the typically cosy way of this miniature industry, he named the company after his suburban home, Ashley, one of a terrace of modest villas in Woodford Green. During the day, completed bodyshells were moved out of the garage and stacked next to the pub so that Pellandine and a couple of men who worked for him could work on the next batch indoors. At night, before everyone adjourned to the Robin Hood, the shells were carried back indoors.

Pellandine went on to conduct experiments with steam cars, a technology which has been an elusive grail for those looking for something cleaner and more sustainable than petrol or diesel. His 'Steam Cat' racer built of Kevlar, the lightweight material also used for bullet-proof uniforms, made a series of attempts in the 1970s on the world speed record for steam cars, which has stood at an impressive 127mph for more than a century, since Fred Marriott's Stanley Steamer tore down Ormond Beach in Florida in 1906. None succeeded, but Pellandine has persisted in his interest and enthused both his son and grandson in the possibilities of steam. The seven Pellandini Minis which reached the market between 1970 and 1974 are largely forgotten, except by enthusiasts who still hunt for any trace or surviving component of them.

Pellandine was a restless character during his business career and he developed the car in Australia, during a spell living in Cherry Gardens near Adelaide, another cosy suburb. Many other Mini variants were born overseas, including a much more successful Australian car marketed as the Morris Mini K, in which K stood for Kangaroo and sales were promoted by the slogan 'A great leap forward'. The model did not actually hop and it retained the traditional round-nose look of Issigonis' original design, but its engine was powered up to 1098cc, which could give passengers a jolt on setting off if the driver was clumsy on the clutch. The car was made between 1969 and 1971 at BMC's factory in Zetland, New South Wales, of which more shortly.

Back at Longbridge, the 1970s saw successively a Mark 3 and Mark 4 of the original Mini, improved to keep pace with increasingly sophisticated rival small cars and in the process losing some of the remaining trademarks of Issigonis' severe virtues. Wind-up windows replaced sliders and door hinges were at last concealed. The car was still hugely popular, but demand began to slide in the face of formidable opposition from the likes of the Ford Fiesta, Renault 5 and Volkswagen Polo. Production of the Mini had finally stopped at Cowley in 1968 and many thought the end had come for the Longbridge line in 1980, when the Austin Mini-Metro, badged simply as mini, appeared. It was officially announced as British Leyland's main small car. The following year was the last that the Mini appeared in the top ten sales list for

British cars, at ninth place to the Metro's fifth. By 1990, when I bought my sons Tom and Olly an *I-Spy Cars* book, the Mini wasn't even included. Mass sales were over but demand for special editions kept production going, and accelerated the little car's gradual shift from a practical runabout in general use to a cherished icon. The trend enjoyed particular success in Japan and put out a marker for what was to come from MINI at Cowley in the future.

These dozens of official varieties, and thousands of individual conversions, saw the Mini establish a remarkably consistent and long-lasting sales success. Steadily the counter ticked: the 500,000th in December 1962 and the 1,000,000th in 1965, a total which doubled by 1969 and trebled in October 1972. Lord Stokes, who was by then as lukewarm about the Mini's future as his predecessor Lord Nuffield had been about the Morris Minor, which he derided as a 'poached egg', unusually agreed to pose beside the 3,000,000th car. A leggy model did the honours for the 4,000,000th in 1976 and Noel Edmonds went to Cowley for the half-billionth ten years later. Possibly still crunching Colin Manders' aspirin, he stood grinning beside it, with its seats still plastiwrapped.

But the other consistent feature of this progress was the red ink on the BMC balance sheets. Mini pricing policy had not changed since Lord ignored Ford's private warning that each car was selling for £30 less than it cost to build. As early as November 1962 *The Times* made the issue public by suggesting that BMC's fall in profits – by nearly half to just £11.5 million on a turnover of £311 million – was not being helped by the financing of the little car. 'The Mini range has certainly proved a success so far as sales are concerned, but the competitive pricing has bitten deeply into profit margins,' the paper commented. It added pointedly that cars with engines of under 1000cc, the market dominated by the Mini, accounted for 60 per cent of BMC's output, compared to 57 per cent in 1960–1 and 43 per cent in 1956–7.

Costs were hard for the company to cut, with the government still requiring a spread of manufacturing to bolster employment as widely as possible. Components came from several different factories in Birmingham and others in Coventry, Castle Bromwich, Oxford and South Wales. It was only in the late 1980s and early '90s, when volume was modest and the big sellers were the de luxe models and limited editions, that the car at last began to make a small profit.

Meanwhile the freelance adaptations got weirder and wilder. Recalling the car's infamous early leaks, one housed a Jacuzzi; three entered an advertising career as realistic, super-sized Outspan oranges and another became a Dalek from that other great survivor from the Sixties, the TV series *Dr Who*. A Traveller had a thatched roof added to its half-timbers, and sprint-shell drag racers were reduced in height to little more than two feet off the ground; one of them, scarcely more than a skateboard with a Mini engine, won Guinness World Records' approval as the lowest car in the world. Mini enthusiasts who wistfully longed for a caravan were offered Little Guy, with TV, a beer pump and a foldaway barbecue as well as two very compact beds. The

Trimini had a single back wheel while the Bodyworks Minidesk didn't move at all. It was designed as the petrolhead's ultimate office dream: the gutted shell of a classic Mini is a desk topped with polished wood and leather, including space for a computer console and keyboard. The boot and bonnet are converted into cupboards for stationery and files.

Equally odd is a stable of peculiarities familiar at summer events; I watched them perform at the *Yorkshire Post*'s classic car show in the grounds of Harewood House in June 2009. There were grass-track racers, double-engine Minis and a push-me-pull-you weld-together which faces both ways. They will run for years to come but arose from an obsession which was triggered thirty years ago by children's TV – an example of the way that the Mini forges on and on. As the team prepared at Harewood, its leader Marco recalled, 'I must have been nine or ten the first time I saw stunt Minis, on *Blue Peter* on our black-and-white TV. Minis when I was growing up were so cool. I remember them on *Grandstand*, always doing the business, winning the races. I grew up with Minis – I went to school in one, I fell out of one. Come to think of it, I was conceived in one. So that's how it all started.' He got into bike-jumping at the same time, persuading his friends to lie down in a line on his family's front lawn, then yanking his pushbike into the air and just clearing them. That inspired him to hold his first show at the age of seven. It raised £17.40 for Guide Dogs for the Blind.

Marco wished he still had his first Mini, a 1963 blue Austin Se7en which he bought for £40 from a midwife in

Bolton. 'It was really basic; you worked the headlamps through a switch in the floor, it had sliding windows and no door handles – you had to stick in a wire to open it. It would be a collector's item now, but unfortunately it got nicked from outside a pub.' It turned up a week later as a write-off in a scrapyard, but Marco got £170 for the wreckage plus a £450 reward from the police who caught the thief and broke up a car-stealing racket as a result. In the old Austin's place, starting off with this little fund and using his father-in-law's garage, he has gradually designed, over seven years, a stunt collection of bright red oddities which spend the year touring Britain's fairgrounds and shows. There's the Bug, a shorty like Holly Brown-Horsley's but with added roller bars, as well as a strengthened floor, extra shock-absorbers and sump guard. Seven feet long, it is handy for doughnuts, 360-degree spins and handbrake turns and fits snugly inside one of the group's Transit vans.

Next up came the Minitour, whose name refers to the Theseus legend – but there the elegant classical references stop. The car has been stripped of everything possible except its 1300cc engine to make it as light but powerful as possible for grass racing, a horrendous display of slides and skids. Beside it, oddest of all, waits the MegaMini itself, facing both ways like the old slate-mine locomotives on the Talyllyn railway in Wales. Four-wheel drive, it has two 1300cc engines like John Cooper's fateful Twini. It can drive either way, with the front-facing engine in first or second gear and the rear one in reverse; or the car can be snapped apart and turned into two bizarre shorties with only front wheels and strengthened rears which can race, or at least slither, separately before being rejoined.

'It's the only vehicle on the planet which can do this,' announced Marco, to no one's surprise, although he acknowledged the source of his inspiration. An escapologist and showman called J.C. Diamond had an act which included a double-ended Mini. As his career came to an end, Marco took over his cars and remade them, strengthening them for the stunt work which Diamond didn't do. The old pro's list of engagements followed and MegaMinis were off. Marco and his friend Wilbur did their first show in Croydon, joining a bill which included the then world's strongest man John Evans, who could carry a Mini on his head. Even the stunt team were awed by this eccentricity, which depended on Evans' 24-inch neck, sturdy posture and ability to stand absolutely still; a slip or twitch might have killed him. Pictures abound of Evans' most famous Mini-balancing, which lasted for thirty-three seconds with a bright red Cooper wobbling slightly above his fringe at the London Studios in May 1999. It got him his place in the *Guinness Book of Records* for the heaviest car ever balanced on a head; and ten years later, at the age of sixty-two, he is still at it. If you have £1,400, he will turn up for your charity do or party in his motor-home truck with its 14ft trailer and lift the Cooper, after a curtain-raiser involving 97 milk crates, 225 pints of beer, a quad bike and a cement mixer. He wittily calls his act The Balance of Power.

'It always had to be a Mini,' he said, when I asked him why he chose the Cooper for his tour de force. 'Runners-up? No, there was only ever the one choice for me. The most famous British car in the world, *The Italian Job*, maximum impact all round. Plus, my first car was a Mini Cooper and I had some crazy drives in it. Come to think of it, I'm in a book called *Celebrity My First Car* and they got me to do a headlift for the launch party at the Trafford Centre in Manchester.' He managed 204 hardback copies of the book, which has his comfy, beaming and Cooper-crushed self on the cover. It went down a storm.

Evans' lifting Cooper isn't the full-scale item, which weighs an impossible 1300 lbs. Instead, he got his red one stripped down to little more than a shell with a motorbike engine which gives a realistically throaty put-put and puffs smoke out of the exhaust as the car teeters. Still, it weighs 25 stone, which is three stone more than he does himself and has guaranteed that a very British record is still retained by a Briton. But for how long? There is every chance that, like the cramming-people-into-a-Mini title, it could fall to an overseas contender; because enthusiasm for the big little car has spread all over the world.

## Chapter Ten
## Near and Far

*'It has re-established English inventive genius.'*
Didier Merlin, *motoring correspondent of*
Le Figaro, *1964*

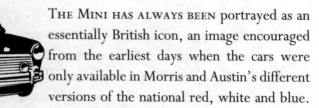

THE MINI HAS ALWAYS BEEN portrayed as an essentially British icon, an image encouraged from the earliest days when the cars were only available in Morris and Austin's different versions of the national red, white and blue. The Union Jack has appeared on wings, mirrors, boots and most commonly the car's roof, as well as in vast mosaic form, made up of hundreds of actual Minis in tableaux at rallies to celebrate the car's growing number of birthdays. But there has always been an international strain to both the story and the legends. Minis have travelled to every country in the world and have been made under licence in more than a dozen. They have had major sales successes, especially in Italy, and sadly missed opportunities, notably in the United States; but they have done the UK's reputation good, particularly in helping to change the stuffy old images of British Empire days.

It is only right for a car which Issigonis' friend Sir Peter

Ustinov described as created by a man who was 'an odd mixture of English, Greek and German, steeped in Turkish olive oil', that there should be more than 110 enthusiasts' and owners' clubs outside the UK. They range from the Mighty Mini Club of Sri Lanka to the online 59 Squadron Mini Nuts which covers scores of countries. The Fabmoc Mini Owners' Club based in Wales and Yorkshire keeps a register of examples spotted abroad, like those people who take a favourite Teddy round the world and photograph it in famous places. In between taking part in Fish and Chip Runs and Moorland and Coast Adventures, to raise money for charity, members have logged four pictures from Australia, three from France and one in the States so far in 2009. A smart green Cooper with racing roundels was flagged down in Botany Bay, a very smart metallic-blue saloon with French number-plates greeted another explorer in a Calais car park, and the American contribution was the only survivor of five Minis used in the film *The Bourne Identity*. They missed E788 XGK though, an eighteen-year-old white saloon (plus Union Jack top of course) which overcame five mountain ranges and three deserts on the Mongol Rally from London to Ulan Bator. 'I don't think Sir Alec Issigonis had the foresight to consider the Mongol Rally when he designed the Mini,' mused Andy Place, who bounced and slithered the 9000 miles with co-driver Jon Batchelor, a former finalist in his university's go-karting competition for first-year students. Their list of breakdowns was as awesome as the obstacles on the rally route, but the Mini's gutsy reputation and, more important, simple mechanics by modern standards, saw them through. The worst moment came when their radiator started leaking on the deserted later stages of the rally in Mongolia itself. With the same nonchalance, Andy recorded: 'We were able to buy some Red Seal which cured the problem, from a small shop in the middle of the Gobi desert.' Meanwhile a Chichester Mini enthusiast, Duncan Mortimer, is doggedly taking his thirty-one-year-old Mini Clubman round the world for the third time to raise money for cancer charities. The first time, he took his Thai-born wife Yuwadee, the second time a friend from Selsey and this time – monitored by a website called Where on Earth is Duncan? with slots reserved for his diary and pictures until July 2010 – he is on his own.

Minis are a regular sight on such epics, including the Mongol and half a dozen other chassis-busting international rallies, and although the annual Arctic run in Canada is a new MINI affair, the classic car has been there too. From the start its makers seem to have pictured the Mini in distant lands. How else, for example, would one of their early modifications succeed? It was a limited edition of the car designed to test competition with 'beach wagons', a genre which stripped down traditional cars by removing their doors and creating something that looked like a high-powered golf-kart. They were more popular around the Mediterranean than in Britain, for obvious reasons, and examples often featured at the Turin motor show where British car-firm executives eyed them wistfully. But the Mini's success from 1961 onwards prompted BMC to build sixteen at Longbridge, adapted by the company's chief stylist into what Lawrence Pomeroy considered 'a most entrancing and elegant car for the use of hotels de grand luxe, which use them to carry customers from the bar to the beach'. Issigonis was evidently happy with this, particularly when one of the beach Minis was requested by Buckingham Palace. A picture survives of him driving a slightly different version, with a boot for picnic hampers, snorkels and flippers. He is giving a cheerful grin. The beach cars were a taster for the Moke which, as we have seen, turned out to be much more suitable for fun on the sand than demanding military operations.

The Mini was also soon franchised out to BMC's factories overseas, with production of the Cooper starting in Australia in 1962. Three years later, the firm announced a deal to build more at Seneffe in southern Belgium. This allowed the Mini to drive through regulations of the then European Economic Community which imposed tariffs on vehicles from non-members such as the UK, and it was followed two months later by a similar arrangement with Innocenti of Milan. This was taking the battle to the heartland of the Fiat Cinquecento, the only previous small car which came near to (but did not equal) the Mini's extraordinary roominess in a confined space. The Italians, whose products included the lastingly successful Lambretta scooter, proved to have more financial nous than the parent company in Britain. They ignored BMC's pricing policy and boldly charged more for their Mini than Fiat were doing for the Cinquecento's more powerful 850 version, their direct competitor. They were confident that the Innocenti

Mini-Minor, as it was branded, offered more and the car bore them out, becoming a lonely little island of profit-ability in the Mini's sea of loss. Soon, some 700 cars were leaving the assembly lines every week, and annual production reached 55,000 in the early 1970s, a market second only to the British home one.

Innocenti's success caught Longbridge's eye. The Italians were encouraged and nurtured until, in 1972, British Leyland bought them out and sent one of its star managers to take charge. Geoffrey Robinson, who was later to make a second albeit rather less successful name in politics, moved from his job as the company's financial controller to take charge in Milan. He saw the huge appeal of the Mini there and launched a drive to up productivity and increase exports to other European countries. The centrepiece was an advanced new Mini Cooper 1300, made possible by a direct deal between Innocenti and John Cooper which had survived the Donald Stokes debacle. The car was an instant success, particularly with the style-conscious Italians, and Robinson did all he could to increase production. Demand constantly stayed ahead of him, and the Innocenti Mini Cooper could have played a significant part in reviving BL's fortunes through sales overseas. But it was too late. The company's loss-making operations in the UK bled it to the point where it was nationalised in 1975 and the new regime abandoned promotion of its foreign plants. Robinson was summoned home to concentrate on Jaguar, where he was also chairman. The following year he entered politics as Labour MP for Coventry North West, later buying the *New Statesman* magazine and becoming Paymaster General in Tony Blair's first government. But the inspiration he showed with the Italian Mini Cooper deserted him in his new profession. He was forced to resign in December 1998 after ill-advisedly loaning his colleague Peter Mandelson £373,000 to buy a house.

The Italian Minis fared better. Innocenti was initially rescued by the Italian government but then joined the illustrious stable of companies assembled by Alejandro de Tomaso, a Formula One racing driver who had fled to Italy in his twenties from his native Argentina where he had been implicated in a plot to overthrow the vanity-ridden dictator General Juan Peron. He also rescued Maserati from bankruptcy and owned the famous coachbuilding firm Ghia. De Tomaso had noted Robinson's flair and enterprise and proved well able to copy it. He escaped dependence on BL by secretly making a deal with the Japanese car firm Daihatsu to provide him every month with 2000 engines which could be fitted into Mini bodies. He had no intention of ending a success story which had seen more than 220,000 Italian Minis sold.

Given a free hand with the Milan factory, he came up with a series of what became known as Inni Minis, boxy perversions of Issigonis' classic shape to the sensitive eye, but cars with guts. They included the 1275cc Mini de Tomaso itself, a sort of Mediterranean Cooper, and had a staying power which saw their successor, the Mini 3, sell well from 1985 until 1993. Available with turbo-charging, and honouring the Mini legend with livery in red, white or blue, the Inni

Minis won the admiration of *Autocar* magazine, which nick-named them 'butch babies'. Testing one of very few which managed to dodge Britain's then protectionist import regulations, the magazine found it 'irresistible, an engaging little car with an on-the-road performance as chirpy as its appearance'. The overall ride might be as noisy and turbulent as a Cooper's at full stretch, but 'there would surely be a market for it as a cult-car appealing both to chic-about-town Chelsea-ites, and "bring-back the Cooper S" enthusiasts'.

Minis made overseas often took different names in the way that the Innocenti cars did, although the muddle of Mini-Minors, Austin Se7ens, Elfs and Hornets in the UK gave the British market no grounds for criticising that. In April 1972 Australian Minis were dispiritingly renamed Leylands, although not for long, and one of the great rarities in the Mini collectors' world is the Venezuelan Cord. The few survivors are the vestigial result of a 'small car' attack on the once wealthy market in Venezuela, which profited greatly from oil in the 1970s but fell on hard economic times in the following decade. American gas-guzzlers went out of favour in a fervour of austerity, reacting against the wastefulness of the 'Saudi-zuela' period, which had seen the prosperous import even basic food products from Miami, including bread. Petrol quadrupled in price and the local car-assembly plants started to look at smaller and more fuel-efficient models. Toyota, Fiat and Renault were all targets but the Mini was in their sights. A businessman called Victor Vargas got together a consortium and bought a licence from Rover to produce up to 5000 of the cars a year, installing

British engines and parts inside fibreglass bodies. The company Facorca (Fábrica Cordillera de Carocerias, which combined with wordplay on the United States' most famous model to give the car its name Cord) would have preferred steel but it was too expensive, and the Venezuelan government insisted that a reasonable percentage of the car should be locally made, rather than just put together from foreign components like a kit.

In the first year from December 1991, 113 Minis left the factory, some travelling to owners as far afield as the Antilles islands. But the original targets were a long way off; production rose to 768 in 1992 but fell back to 391 the following year. The car was certainly economical compared to the Venezuelan elite's old Cadillacs and Chevvies, but it was a bit basic. The 'luxury' model, known as the Mini Cord DB, had leather trim, spotlights and air-conditioning, but it wasn't terribly gutsy. The troubles were compounded by Venezuela's increasingly disastrous economy and personal quarrels between Vargas' business partners. Like others before them, Facorca thought 'Cooper' and did a deal for tuning-up kits with the John Cooper Works, but it was too late. The Mini hadn't taken off and neither had the Venezuelan economy more widely. The little outpost made twenty-four cars in 1994 and fifteen the next year, and then closed down. It has the melancholy distinction of being the smallest commercial run of the car in history.

Its story was briefer but perhaps not as strange as the Mini-building episode in the small and beautiful port of Arica, on the edge of the Atacama desert in northern Chile.

The town's attractions include a British connection, one of several spurious graves of Sir Francis Drake (who was actually buried at sea in a lead coffin off the Caribbean coast of Panama, thousands of miles away). Its cathedral is unusual too, a pink and white prefabricated iron concoction designed by Gustave Eiffel, no less. The method of building was appropriate because, between 1964 and 1974, a group of factories worked under licence, first assembling imported Minis and then marrying British components to locally made fibreglass bodies to produce a Chilean version of the European icon of cool.

The initiative began after the World Cup football final was held in Chile in 1962, a much-publicised, global event which stimulated demand for modern products such as televisions, dishwashers and of course cars. Arica was chosen for a foreign car-assembly factory because of its very remoteness; the hope was that new industry there would nurture secondary suppliers and lift the whole regional economy. BMC was not the only big car-making name which took the bait; Chevrolet and Ford signed up for assembly packages too. The financial systems were curious, with the Chilean government's enthusiasm for encouraging car plants leading to twenty-two different factories, and in these the old BMC weakness of dividing its product by marque was faithfully replicated. Three factories had BMC licences, one producing both Austin Se7ens and Morris Mini-Minors while the others stuck to Morris only, one of them running an assembly line for Morris Minors even shorter than Facorca's Mini run; only six were made. Mini production in Arica was also modest but not as Lilliputian as this. In 1965 the various factories made 180 and by 1968 this had risen to 879. The shift to fibreglass bodies upped the total to 2,356 in 1972.

Revolutionary economic changes by Chile's socialist president Salvador Allende, who won power the following year, led to BL's withdrawal, although the country continued to be a reasonably good market for finished cars imported from Britain. Arica was left with deserted factories and piles of fibreglass body shapes which were curiously familiar to the occasional British tourist who had come in search of Drake's non-grave or the Eiffel cathedral. Stories live on, too, of British Leyland's brief attempt to set up another factory assembling MG 1300s out of a mixture of Chilean fibreglass bodies and British cars. The project was dogged by local rivalry, to the extent that its senior staff carried Sten guns on long journeys on the largely empty local roads. One of them, driving a Mini, was tailed by a Chilean official whom he lured into a trap worthy of *The Italian Job*. Gunning his engine, he shot his car through a very narrow opening off the road. The tail followed in a much wider Ford, which squashed itself between the walls and was jammed to a halt.

Although pint-sized, these South American operations left a lasting legacy of enthusiasm among local Mini owners. Looking particularly modest against the gigantic landscape of the Andes, the little cars still regularly rally and hold Mini meets. The title for the southernmost regular gathering of Mini owners is claimed by the Chilean city of Rancagua, capital of O'Higgins province, named after one of the country's liberators of Irish descent. Rancagua Ministas form one of a dozen groups of fans of the car in the country, headed by Austin CL, which describes itself as '*El Club de Minis mas grandes de Chile*'. This hardly needs translating, any more than the eager welcome from the Club Dinastia Cooper to a function in the beauty spot of Cajon del Maipo in the central Andes, to celebrate both the car's birthday and the club's: '*Invitamos todos los minimaniacos a celebrar con nostros nuestro primo anniversario.*'

The Chilean clubs also maintain good contact with their counterparts in Spain, where enthusiasm for the Mini is equally lively. A flavour can be had from a YouTube clip posted from Leganes on the outskirts of Madrid, where the Club Issigonis held revels in 2008. Linked in a circle in Calle General Aranda outside a Guinness bar, a score of young club members dance and sing a catchy Mini-related song, all wearing dark Oxford blue T-shirts with a Mini pictured in light Cambridge blue on their breast pockets and backs. Beside them, as they gambol about and a young blonde tootles away on a plastic green and yellow trumpet, stands a Cooper painted in the same livery of contrasting blues. *Olé!*

Spain was the third country to start Mini-building, when BMC got together in 1965 with a company in Pamplona to set up Authi, Automoviles de Turismo Hispano Ingleses, to get round the strict rules of General Francisco Franco's protectionist dictatorship. These were so harsh, compared to most such international collaborations which see car parts provided by both participating countries, that everything in the Authi Minis had to be sourced in Spain. Even the engines were made there, at a factory specially built near Santander. This gave the cars the curious distinction of being the only Minis in the world not to have Bill Cull's wonderful Rzeppa joints; the Generalissimo could not find a Spanish factory able to cope with their exceptionally exact engineering, which in Britain was done on machine tools which Cull had also designed. Authi Minis therefore have simpler universal joints, and surviving examples should probably not be driven so far or fast as the 'real' thing. Given the desire of collectors for oddities, however, the mechanical shortfall may add to their market value.

The Spanish plant ran well in spite of these shortcomings, and produced Minis until May 1975, when a Damask Red saloon was the last to leave the line. Although the operation never reached its target of 55,000 cars a year, it did reasonably in comparison with Innocenti, and actually rather well when compared with other Spanish companies building rival cars. The young people bobbing in Leganes (whose youthful Anglo culture also includes the world's only street named after the Australian rock band AC/DC) testify to the lasting appeal of El Mini, and car production still continues at the Pamplona factory, by SEAT, Sociedad Espanola de Automoviles de Turismo, who bought the plant from BL in 1975. Now part of Volkswagen, the former Mini shops turn out Polos.

The sale came in the year of disaster for British Leyland, finally overwhelmed by its long-standing financial troubles, amid high inflation, a continuing international oil crisis and the sour legacies of the three-day week. The company went bankrupt and was subsequently nationalised, with effects felt at all its foreign subsidiaries and partnerships. The last annual accounts showed a loss of £123 million and the firm had to make provision for more than £60 million to cover the cost of 16,000 redundancies in four countries. It did not go easily. Authi was sold successfully, but there was anger and bitterness in Milan. Innocenti under Geoffrey Robinson had expanded to employ 5000 workers by 1974, when its Mini production topped 61,000 cars. By early in 1975, there were 8,000 of these standing in the car parks by the plant reserved for unsold vehicles, and the following autumn there was serious industrial unrest over a proposal to make 1,500 staff redundant.

Australia was also in trouble, in spite of sprightly attempts to market the Moke, including a film made in 1971 with the commentary in French – apart from words such as 'hard top' and 'piggy back'. The latter comes in a section of the film which shows one of the lesser-known assets of the jeeplet: the way that one can carry another on its 'back', making for extra room on car transporters or trains. Another version featured in the film actually dispensed with the need for trains altogether; it was mounted on engine wheels and sped along tracks in Queensland under its own power. Other Mokes – *inspirés de la fameuse Mini*' as the commentary observes – chase criminals with New South Wales police on board, fight bush blazes with the state firefighters and haul an equally midget seed-sower around an outback farm. Production of these continued until 1982 but the wider range of Minis limped on in Australia only until October 1978 when the New South Wales plant closed after finishing its 176,284th car.

The focus of discontent then moved to Belgium, where Seneffe learned in November the same year that production of the car was to be cut by nearly a third. Just over two years later BL closed the factory altogether, with the loss of 2,200 jobs and another 225 in Oxford where kits of parts for the Belgian plant were assembled. The British ambassador, Sir Peter Wakefield, was summoned by the Belgian prime minister as workers occupied the plant and blocked BL's nearby European distribution centre with the aim of holding some 3,500 new cars there hostage. There was a keen and justifiable resentment; unlike strike-torn Longbridge and Cowley, Seneffe's seventeen years had not seen a single walkout and productivity had risen year by year.

Except at Innocenti, the popularity of the Mini never made much difference to the saga of declining fortunes, because of the underpricing which had been part of its story from the start. But now it began to lose ground in terms of its merits too; by 1975 it was looking all of its sixteen years in the face of newer rivals. *Car* magazine wrote candidly: 'The Mini is an embarrassment. It is painfully out of date in just about every respect except price, but will continue to find adherents regardless; it may not be a good car anymore, but it is a convenient one that the vast majority understand.' Mini-making continued overseas in a sporadic way, including the production of Mokes in Portugal until the 1990s, but the glory days, and hopes, had gone.

The brightest of them had actually succumbed seven years earlier when a gradually developing market in the United States was abruptly cut short by stricter federal safety standards for cars. The Mini's design had not sufficiently taken into account the trend towards such controls, and the growing concern about emissions from exhausts, particularly overseas where such measures could be convenient as a disguise for protectionism – remember the long battle fought by the United States aircraft industry against Concorde. Issigonis was notoriously dubious about even seatbelts, taking the purist view of an extremely experienced driver that safety should lie in the hands of the man or woman at the wheel. Rather than wanting to protect passengers from disaster, as do today's strengthened, airbag-equipped and therefore larger cars, he believed that disaster was something a safe driver would not encounter. In the United States, in particular, this attitude was a disaster in itself.

It played a part in the fact that the Mini's apparently impressive total of more than 5,300,000 sales is dwarfed by the VW Beetle's final total of over 21 million. Had the little car been safer and cleaner and a little bit bigger, it might have taken a healthy slice of the Beetle's market; it could perhaps have added the Hollywood role of Herbie to its laurels from *The Italian Job*. When the first Minis were shipped across the Atlantic less than a year after the launches in Longbridge and Cowley, they undercut the VW substantially: $1,295 to $1,675. Although smaller, they could equal a Beetle for speed on a straight stretch of road and far outmatched it on corners. The American motoring press loved the new arrival. Gordon Wilson, who had been the first US journalist to test the Beetle, admiringly described the Mini's appearance in *Motor Trend*: 'With its tiny wheel stuck out on the four corners, it looks broadshouldered, muscular and sure-footed.' *Sports Graphic* gushed eagerly: 'It spells FUN and ECONOMY in capitals and has more surprises than a visit to Disneyland.'

The marketing was not up to scratch, however, in spite of the unpaid help given by a number of celebrity equivalents of the stars who were driving Minis round swinging London. Steve McQueen was the best known, nipping along Los Angeles' freeways in a Cooper as often as he did in his Jaguar XK-SS or Ferrari 250 Lusso. But that couldn't hold off the legislators, and the Mini's seven years on sale in the States saw safety regulations relentlessly tightened, preceded by suggestions in the US media that such a tiny car was inherently dodgy. The federal government took the same view, and in 1967 the Mini became illegal on US roads simply because its wheelbase was too short to meet the new standards. Size mattered. For a while longer, the cars could have got by on emissions and safety rules, but BMC did not have the capacity to stretch them. It had altered the lights and radiator grille of the Morris Minor to allow that car to continue selling in the States when federal laws were similarly toughened in 1949, but the Mini's shortcomings were too fundamental. Remaining models were withdrawn with fewer than 10,000 sold, and even today, when classic cars can escape regulations in the

US if they are twenty-five years old, the Mini is a very rare sight there. Your best chance, like the Welsh and Yorkshire foreign Mini spotters of Fabmoc, is to find a cinema re-running *The Bourne Identity*.

There was still a foreign surprise to come, however, from those other devotees of cool European icons, the Japanese. The Mini had been exported there in the 1970s but trade stopped when Japanese legal demands on imported vehicles made the game no longer worth the candle. After a decade, the system was relaxed a little and in the 1980s so few obstacles remained that the car became a minor cult in Tokyo and other major cities. BL held a glitzy relaunch of a modified model, with flared wheel arches and headrests, and in 1981 clocked up 1000 sales. The cars were adapted by Carbodies, better known as the principal maker of London taxis, with catalytic exhaust converters added to conform with Japanese emission rules.

Special editions and a love of oddities have since swollen Japanese interest to the level of fervour they show for Beatrix Potter, or the enthusiasm for the Brontës which has led to the erection of direction signs in Japanese in Haworth. Their bible is *Mini Freak*, produced by the Japanese Mini Specialists' Association, which has thrived so much that it changed in 1999 from an amateur bunch of enthusiasts into a business corporation. The introduction to *Mini Freak* sets out the gospel:

> Mini. 50 years from birth, still attracting many people with its pre-production story, great history, and heart-appealing

excellent styling. For the existence of Mini beyond time, we at the JMSA place this little car as our 'legacy of the motoring world.' We'd like to keep this legacy running as long as possible. Like the Mini of 1959 is still on the road, we'd also like to see the Minis of 2000 on the road in 2050. For JMSA, we believe that Minis must be driven well at any period of time. We protect Minis so that they may still be used every day.

The sense of gleeful pleasure in the car is common to other enthusiasts in distant places, and among people whose countries were at odds with Britain in the older generation's lifetime, with no special reason to be fond of the Union Jack. Japan is one example, Germany another; the country now has ownership of the new MINI and is understandably proud of its success. Still, it is a pleasure to see an online Union Jack rippling away on the home page of enthusiasts in Bremen and area. '*Herzlich wilkommen beim Mini Fun-Club,*' reads the greeting alongside, and all the little red Minis which fill gaps in the pages and form click-on links have Union Jacks painted on their sides as well. They were there at the International Mini Meet in Longbridge in August 2009, along with Mini Club Bavaria, Mini Club Zagreb, Minis of Le Mans and dozens of others – Hungary, Turkey, the States, you name it – including Malta Mini Owners, who are my favourite because their island is small and plucky, like Chloe Greenall's Mini Cooper, and it has done so much to keep some of Britain's oldest buses in daily use.

There's an offbeat link with British Leyland; and just as the trumpeting, creaking yellow charabancs still grind round the Triton fountain outside Valetta's main city gate in Floriana, so plenty of Minis negotiate the often Moke-worthy local roads. The scale of devotion to them is shown in an online hymn of praise to MMM 850, the club's featured car, for the get-together in Birmingham. Its owner remembers it as a boy; he had a particular fascination with the floor starter button, and spent years negotiating with a later owner to buy the car back. The other man was equally in love with it, but finally agreed to part with it on condition that it was fully restored to its saleroom condition back in the mid-1960s. The condition has been met, and the Mini now gleams in Clipper Blue, with a replacement for the Les Leston racing driver's steering wheel which the owner's father bought in the 1960s, and – the only possible cause of disapproval by the shade of Issigonis – a period radio which has been wired in. 'It was our family's first car and pride and joy when I was a little boy,' says its citation. 'Now I intend to keep it forever because it is a dream come true. I would not sell it for anything in the world. "Till death do us part."'

Britain's attitude to all this global warmth is generally benign, until a famous competition enters the picture. In 2008 the title for assembling the largest number of the cars in one place was snatched by the Dutch, who managed to get 884 together at the International Mini Meeting in Leylstad and to drive them in convoy for 20 kilometres. The enormous crawl, which earned each participant a com-memorative plate from a ferry company, was admired by all, but British fans were determined to get the record back. So they did, assembling 1,585 Minis at Crystal Palace to mark the 50th anniversary in 2009 and then driving off in another enormous crocodile, choreographed so carefully that the first fifty cars were consecutively dated 1959 to 2000, in terms of when they left the factory.

One outpost has gone unmentioned: the Antarctic, which had seen its first car in 1907, when a four cylinder Arrol Johnston accompanied Sir Ernest Shackleton's expedition. A Mini duly followed the great explorers into the white wilderness. Mounted on caterpillar tracks, which rolled round three wheels on either side of the car, it was called the Mini-trac and was based at Australia's Wilkes research base in 1965. A photograph taken by one of the scientists shows it trundling along through the snow in front of Wilkes' simple wooden hut, with its driver apparently scanning the dashboard anxiously.

The Mini-trac was designed by an engineer called Terry O'Hare at a workshop in the inappropriately named Melbourne suburb of Sunshine. He imported snowmobile parts from Sweden and Canada but wanted the Mini version to be as authentically close to the original – a standard 850cc model – as possible. The car's engine drove the twin-belt rubber matting which gave the tracks grip on the snow. The result gave good service, replacing a couple of VW Beetles which had been adapted in the same curious way. As for the opposite pole, that has its own annual Arctic Mini Run every February, slithering along sections of routes such as the Trans-Labrador Highway. But look closely. The participants' cars are called Minis, but they are not as we have known have known them. Welcome to the car's latest chapter: the age of the MINI in capital letters. And prepare to consider these questions: have the Germans of BMW found a way of taking our accident-prone icon, with its false premise, muddled start and history of depending on luck, into an actual, highly organised money-earner? And are we – goodness! – learning to love ... no, not that, but at least to *quite like* what they have done?

## Chapter Eleven
## New MINI

IN THE 1990S, MEDICAL OPINION in Britain woke up to the fact that people were getting alarmingly fat. Obesity became a watchword and a media concern. Reporters like myself were despatched to interview unfortunate children who were trying to improve their startlingly ponderous figures at 'fat camps'. No one – apart from an American group which tried to enlist sympathy for large victims of what they named 'sizeism' – thought that this was a good thing.

The new MINI therefore started at something of a public-relations disadvantage. Placed alongside an Issigonis original, it was uncomfortably similar to a fat camp child standing next to a more normally shaped one. Where the original Mini is small and neat, with sides running trimly down in an almost vertical line, the new one has a bulbous skirt and a plump bottom. The classic car's ten-inch wheels look like black dolly mixtures next to its successor's standard big tyres. Where the original has the neatest of bonnets like a retrousse nose, the MINI has a snout which ends in two large and oddly tilted headlamp 'eyes'. Everything is maxi, not mini. The record for the number of people who can be crammed inside went straight to nineteen, and has now reached twenty-four.

I didn't like it, at least in comparison with the famous car whose name it carries, and nor did thousands of 'old Mini' partisans, who went to the lengths of organising campaigns against the travesty, as they saw it, of this metal balloon presuming to inherit the glorious past. The Original Mini Owners Club on Bebo is one of dozens of websites involved, contrasting the two cars on its home page and asking: 'From this … to this … Where did it all go wrong?' Below, a spoof Lord's Prayer enlists divine help against the invader, ending 'for Thine is the Mini (the original one), for ever and ever, amen'. Another site, bluntly called IhatetheBMWMINI, comes and goes, but was accessible when I tried it in June 2009 under the appropriate host address of Fatblokeracing. Its webmaster was very excited by an online game called Chuck the Small Car which involves digitally smashing a new MINI about. He had found it in turn on the site of Notts About Minis, a club whose referendum on whether to admit MINI owners resulted in a vote that Yes, they could come to meetings, but only so long as they owned a classic Mini as well and didn't bring their new one (which the club calls a 'small BMW') with them.

The Bean family who shopped in IKEA with me at the start of this book get waved at by MINIs when they are out in Merlin, but they only reluctantly respond, unlike the waves, grins and beams which break out when a classic Mini tootles past. You still occasionally see classic Minis with window stickers saying 'You don't have to have a big one to be happy' or 'Contains no BMW additives'. And yet ... As the new MINIs have settled in, they have started to become a little more familiar and, at least in comparison with the four-by-four tanks which some town-dwellers still persist in buying, even to seem relatively compact. There looks to be more variety among them, too, than you see in most types of car; and finally, in the last couple of years, don't their numbers seem to have grown? They have. In 2007, the MINI factory in Cowley at Oxford, which makes only the car and no other marques, was the third most productive in Britain. In 2008, it leap-frogged over Honda in Derbyshire, passed the 1,500,000th MINI mark and is now second only to the huge Toyota works at Sunderland. The car certainly makes money, unlike its predecessor, and its range is expanding. At the Frankfurt Motor Show in September 2009, BMW launched a pair of two-seaters, the Coupe and the Roadster, and suggested they would bring more than a thousand new jobs to Cowley. The recession's savage effect on the motor trade had led to 850 job losses at the MINI plant six months earlier, but there was an echo of Suez in the hard times. Small cars bucked the trend as the year went on, and by September most of those laid off were back at work.

So have the Germans pulled off, commercially, the trick which the original Mini, for all its marvellous engineering and iconic name, never managed? The answer lies at the former Pressed Steel Fisher site on the Oxford ring road, which once turned out body panels for Rolls Royce as well as the Oxfords and Minors of Morris Motors. Today, the sprawl of buildings is notable for huge signs saying 'MINI' and full-size fibreglass replicas of the BMW version perched on roofs and stuck sideways on walls, their tyre-tracks looping back to a heroic mural. Next to them is a three-storey billboard saying 'MADE in Oxford', and beside that 'SOLD in' above colour reproductions of seventy-five national flags, in alphabetical order from Albania to Uruguay.

These are also on the wall in the reception building for visitors, and I started puzzling out some of the less familiar ones while I waited to be collected for a tour of the plant. What was the combination of white and mauve, separated by a jagged line like an apprentice's indenture? Which country flies a red flag with a yellow emblem which looks part star, part flower and part aeroplane propeller? There were two bored-looking young women manning the reception desk, so I told them what I was doing. Immediately, one of them beamed and slid me a photocopy of the flag collection, complete with a line printed at the bottom saying: 'We hope this answers your question but please ask if you need any more information.'

I didn't. The flags were Qatar and Hong Kong, the latter with MINIs already making up two per cent of its car pool, which isn't bad. But how Germanically well organised! How BMW! This is a factory whose staff – known as associates rather than workers – operate in a logical and thoroughly thought-through system. No detail is ignored. It is not like the chaotic days of BMC and British Leyland at all. But there are links to the past. The other decorative feature of the minimalist reception was a blown-up photograph of a blue MINI Cooper with raffish Union Jacks on its roof and wing mirrors – and, with that practical German side again, the registration number OX4 6NL to remind visiting reps and business contacts of the plant's postcode.

Within minutes I was en route to the plant offices with John Hawkins, now in his thirty-seventh year of making cars at Cowley, to meet his boss Angela Stangroom, who heard the call of the Mini when she was only five years old. 'If I opened my bedroom windows on a balmy summer evening,' she said, thinking back to her childhood in Northfields, the neighbouring suburb to Longbridge, 'I could hear the stamping shop pounding away.' 'Whoom! Whoom!' broke in John enthusiastically; he also remembered the din of the panel hammers, a sound as unforgettable as the farting exhaust of a Morris Minor. Stangroom decided to skip university and joined the Longbridge plant as a business trainee, working a sandwich course of college sessions with jobs all over the factory.

So she and John are old British Leyland hands, and that is true of many of the people who make the MINI. Tensions between the old car and its successor seldom surface in conversation; associates can look out of their north-facing windows and see what has happened to the main Morris and later BMC works, where the old Mini assembly line used to be. The entire, vast complex has been demolished and replaced by a business park, surrounding a needle-shaped obelisk in memory of what was once there. They are glad to be carrying on the tradition and to have jobs making cars. The hole in Longbridge's heart is far worse, with the Nanjing motor company only producing a score or so of its new MG TF per week in the last working section of what was once an even larger plant. 'A lot of associates still commute from Longbridge every day, up and down the M40,' says John.

It was the hope of keeping such traditions going which led to a general welcome when, in 1994, BMW took over the Rover and Mini remnants of BL. The company's unhappy traditions had continued after its nationalisation in 1975 and it was almost subsumed into Honda during Margaret Thatcher's corner-shop economy. One of the hopes with BMW was that the prospect of an entirely new Mini, which was regularly raised during the 1980s and '90s, might become a reality. A happy coincidence encouraged optimism: the chairman of BMW at the time of the takeover was Bernd Pischetsrieder, Issigonis' cousin through his German mother's side. He was brought up to call the designer Uncle Alec, and he fell in love with the Mini Cooper, as the ultimate in car design, in his teens.

Pischetsrieder encouraged a debate within BMW about how a new Mini might look: whether to copy the old as faithfully as new technology allowed, or to strike out in a wholly different direction. Famous names such as the Morris Minor had been passed from one sort of car to a completely unrecognisable successor. On the other hand, the new Volkswagen Beetle, launched in 1998, was a recognisable updating of the famous original. Drawing-board suggestions included micro-versions resembling the Smart car as well as much larger designs. Among those most interested was a BMW designer called Frank Stephenson, who shared with Issigonis a cosmopolitan background. His father was Norwegian, his mother Spanish and he was brought up in Morocco where Stephenson senior worked for Boeing. Until the age of seven, his primary languages were Arabic and French and he completed his education in California, at the Art Center School of Design in Pasadena.

He had always liked the Mini and he naturally threw himself into the discussions of a new model. One evening, he went back to his flat in Munich and sat down at the kitchen table to think the challenge through one more time. He had a pencil but no notebook, so he pulled off a couple of sheets of kitchen paper. Then he thought back to 1969 and how a Mini might have been redesigned then, given the constraints of technology at the time. He sketched it out. Then he did the same for 1979 and 1989. Several things were consistent to the three sketches. There were the upright sides to the windows of the passenger compartment; there was the small nose of a bonnet; and there was the smiley face, the one which Peter Ustinov compared to Issigonis' own for its air of knowing innocence.

From this emerged the clever pastiche of the classic car which the new MINI suggests, albeit in its obese and not-at-all miniature form. Like the New Beetle before it and the successor to the Fiat Cinquecento later, the shape suggests inheritance and similar genes. Nothing else about it is inherited; Bill Cull's amazing joints have long since been replaced by a more modern wonder called the McPherson Strut, and Alec Moulton's suspension has been bettered. But when the elderly John Cooper was invited to see the new design not long before his death, his reaction was: 'It's a Mini.' And that is how you feel as the big doors swing shut behind you in Cowley's modern version of Roy, Trevor and Colin's old Longbridge Body and Whites shop.

The unpainted sections of door, boot and bonnet are all recognisable, and Christian Schoerwerth, who shows us round, enjoys passing on their nicknames. A natural enthusiast, he points out the Swan's Neck, an attachment linked to the MINI's front fender, the Map of Africa, which looks just so, and the Donkey's Tail, which slides some-where I couldn't quite fathom into the overall shape.

The huge building is a world away from the days of Roy & Co, with their snow-covered rusting panels brought in from the Boneyard and Sailor Jack having his hangover kip behind the paint ovens. Purpose-built in 1995 after BMW first moved in, it is the home of 500 robots, which pick up body parts and slot them together, automatically spotting the joints with red laser guides, welding them and then checking their work with sonic beams. The clutter and busyness inside mean that the scale is best seen in the reception lobby. An aerial photo there shows the full sprawl of the building, next to a companion picture of the MINI pressing plant in Swindon, where doors, bonnets and other panels are stamped and cut out from huge, initial spirals of rolled steel.

Properly known as Technik Oxford 2, MINI's Body and

Whites had a curious cradling. It was originally intended to put together panels for the Rover 75, which BMW was going to build at Cowley, and paint in the equally vast building next door, which is the size of sixteen football pitches. The new MINI was destined for Longbridge, which Pischetsrieder saw as both the spiritual and practical home of the old car. Issigonis' workshop was still standing in 1995, and all Mini production had moved there as long ago as 1968. The car was still being made there and many of those working on it had done so for years. Tradition and expertise went hand in hand.

But Byzantine negotiations with the British Government forced a last-minute change of plan. Longbridge's valuable development site was put up for auction, and BMW pulled out of Rover and retreated to Oxford with the MINI. For several days lorries loaded with the contents of the respective factories streamed past one another in a giant swap – the biggest civil-engineering project at the time apart from the Millennium Dome. Events were so sudden that about 1000 MINIs were actually made at Longbridge before the changeover. In years to come, collectors will research the relevant engine and chassis numbers and seek them out.

Body and Whites has the air of a massive manufacturing enterprise – not the noise of a textile mill but the drama of sparks cascading from welds as the robots move sinuously around. Coloured a uniform orange, like a science-fiction version of a human workforce, they pick up doors, bonnets and wings with lobster claws and move them into position. 'Their movements are almost human too,' I suggested to

Christian. 'They are literally human in a way,' he replied. 'They've got 20,000 different options programmed in, many copied from us.' On cue, one of the smaller robots tucked a panel under its arm, while another reached carefully inside a MINI shell to carry out a hidden weld.

We clambered up a flight of steps to a sort of conning tower, reassuringly Sellotaped with scraps of paper giving the mobile-phone numbers of real humans, of whom there were few to be seen. The synchrony of the robots below was mesmerising, like a mechanical ballet as seven of them ganged up on the dismembered carcass of a new MINI and pieced it together. 'There are 4,500 spot welds inside each car,' said Christian, with a tone of awe at something he sees every working day. The process takes four and a half hours per car, and excited buyers can check out the progress of their model online.

Still riveted, as one of the big robots took a small component in its pincers as nonchalantly as if it was a morsel of fish, we moved on to watch the almost complete body shells creep along a conveyor to have their roofs welded on. The cars come in a mixture as they used to in the Longbridge shop, scheduled according to customers' or dealers' orders – a Cooper followed by an ordinary saloon and then a topless convertible. The robots in charge of the roof finish the saloon and then go inert and silent. 'Their programme's told them the convertible's next,' Christian explained. 'No roof needed.'

There's a tangy smell of burnt zinc from all the welds as the next of the day's 350 cars slides into the roof section. In the building's own roof, up above, enough spare stock is shunted into waiting lines – 380 car shells, enough to give the plant two days' grace if there's any delay in getting deliveries from Swindon or contractors. We nipped between two showers of sparks and there! Some human beings at last. Each MINI has to be twisted on its side by the equivalent of an enormous barbecue skewer so that workers can reach inside to carry out specialised $CO_2$ welds. The car needs 180 of these and the German-made Kuka robots can't do that. Not yet, anyway.

Done if not dusted, the complete body shells are lifted by more robots onto a shuttle, a process known as lift-and-shift in the rhyming slang of the factory; other examples include splash-and-dash, the final squirt of petrol into the fully assembled MINIs to get them on to the car transporters. Each robot can lift 210 kilos, which comfortably covers the finished shell of the bodywork. As we leave, out into the car park slumbering in June sunshine, one picks up a shell and holds it out for a manual inspection, one of the regular quality-control checks of the overall fit.

The robots could go on for days, with occasional checks, and the human hours are long too. The MINI associates work either of two eleven-hour shifts with a twenty-minute break every two hours plus half an hour for lunch. A halt in the gentle movement of the track taking the growing bodyshells round unsettled Christian. 'Perhaps a rest break?' he speculated. But then with a soft clunk and shudder, the cars are on the move again. So are we, with final thanks and a last bit of technological guile, a foam pad fitted to each shell which hardens in the paint ovens and prevents a tinny tone on the car's internal sound system. And Issigonis banned radios …

Next stop, the actual assembly line; the paint shop is a 'clean' area so visitors don't get to go in there. So on to Technik Oxford 4, where our guide Ian Cummings was waiting. He reminisced to us about his family's Cowley heritage. 'My Grandad was actually a driver for Lord Nuffield before the war, but he fell out with Lady N, which apparently happened quite a lot. He went off to the RAF but came back after the war to work in the factory. Dad was there too, back from the Navy and working in health and safety, and when he got home, Mum went into the works on the twilight shift. She worked on the Rexi seat covers of the Mini, though she always said she wasn't very good at sewing. But perhaps in the Mini, which was all so basic, that didn't really show.'

Ian's empire, like Christian's, is completely different from that of his Dad's day. There are no cramped assembly pits to get at the chassis and wheels. Instead the cars gently rotate on another giant spit while workers slot in and fix the necessaries. No one has to walk backwards while sorting out the front of the car; the whole assembly-line track moves gently along, with the fitters – who, in another radical change from the old days, now include plenty of women – step on and off as the work requires.

This is a much more human place. Just a few robots stand in a cluster, looking heavily outnumbered, to carry out window-glueing and sealing. In place of the orange Kuka groups in Body and Whites, assembly-line technicians work up to seven at a time on each car. Here are the 20,000 movements programmed into the robots, but for real. Even with the MINI's much increased size, the men and women manage elegant gymnastics as one tightens bolts at the rear while a second fits in carpets and a third makes adjustments to the instrument panel. Towards the end of the line, crews are given lights as the car interiors fill up with gear and, in the relative darkness of the workshop, the working space gets harder to see. Each fitting section of the long journey through the shop is timed at sixty-eight seconds, and workers sit inside the cars at several stages as they creep along. Towards the end, just before the splash-and-dash fuelling with petrol or diesel, a few more robots appear, working on the underneath of the car, but it is humans, two associates with electric screwdrivers checking joints on top, who finish the job off.

The line draws on a network of outside suppliers, whose lorries park outside the building at intervals, feeding in products from engines to windscreen wipers, each bar-coded in a time sequence which fits component to intended car when required. Style governs the appearance of the smallest things. Watching the process, John Hawkins can't help repeating the old quip of Morris and Austin workers about their great rival: 'Tin and board make Ford.' There's none of that here. A chart by the main doors shows the journey each MINI makes from its entry as a painted body shell to the Doors Off section (they are removed to help easy access), then through sunroof, engine, seats, lights, wheels and splash-and-dash, until the final area, Doors Back On.

And here is a very significant panel of information for visitors: 'No two MINIs are alike,' it says. There are literally millions of alternatives available. For the exterior, you can pick from 319 options and inside from even more, currently 372. This has been central to the making of the MINI, and it goes back, like the car's evocative shape, to its illustrious predecessor. What made the headlines in the earliest days and lifted the Mini from its torpid post-launch sales? The individual approach of those celebrity customers, Peter Sellers with his painted wicker and George Harrison with the cobra coiled below the petrol-tank cap. The original design team at BMW hit on the idea of bespoke cars for a mass market; not in the hugely expensive sense of making major alterations, or adjusting the bonnet section, which saves a lot of money by being common to all the current lines of MINIs, from convertible to Cooper. But in small but personal choices, such as the colour, lighting and roof decals. Touches which revive the old Mini trick of a mass-produced car tweaked slightly by each owner, in the way that children in school uniform find a cunning method of adjusting it or wearing it in a way which looks ever so slightly different.

You don't even have to buy a MINI to enjoy this. You can log on to the company's site, click 'Design your MINI' and have a happy time with the help of 'Tips for the Car Configurator'. Pick the standard MINI hatch, for example, and immediately you get a choice of seven alternatives, ranging from £12,345 for the basic MINI 1 to £16,580 for a MINI Cooper S. Pick the standard, for economy's sake, and up come ten colours and seven wheel hubs, ten upholstery alternatives and four different trims. Things widen out under Optional Equipment, where extra costs also kick in, from a £75 Bluetooth connection to run-flat tyres for £845. As you click, the price on the screen ratchets up; in a matter of minutes I had hiked my virtual MINI up to £20,040, and that was without a first-aid kit and red triangle, not to mention something called Bi-Xenon headlights and a passenger seat-height adjuster.

As you can see, some of the customisation is as standard as on any car, even if MINI has come up with a stylish and entertaining alternative to thumbing through a showroom brochure and picking a colour with a pushy dealer. But the online list also points up another clever move by the car's German owners. From the moment they took charge of the marque, they were determined to end the twenty-five-year breach with John Cooper. Oxford sells more Coopers than standard MINIs and the range on offer on the Make Your Own Mini website reflects that skew. The choice of basic hatchbacks has two MINI 1s and five Coopers; both convertibles are Coopers and so are three of the four cars in the Clubman range. On top of this there are three more powerful, more expensive too at between £21,225 and £23,475, and branded as John Cooper Works. Plenty of buyers appreciate the extra power beneath the bonnet, but the real attraction of the name is fashion: a John Cooper Works MINI makes the same statement as a Prada dress or Moschino handbag. The Germans priced it accordingly and pulled off the trick which the original Mini never managed:

creating a car that customers want so much, they will pay pretty much whatever they are asked.

The Coopers had survived after the breach with BL through a mixture of car dealerships and their legendary reputation for fine-tuning apparently ordinary cars. In one typical adventure, they produced an upgrading kit for Japanese enthusiasts during the 1980s vogue for Minis in the Far East, which sold brilliantly. They had been approached by a Japanese company which wanted them to 'Cooper' Minis on a large scale, something supported by BL's people in Japan but refused by the company's HQ in Britain. In the end, and rather grudgingly, Longbridge acknowledged that a market existed and asked for a similar upgrading kit to be available in Britain. It led to a limited edition of 1000 Mini Coopers which sold out immediately, and in the last years of the old Mini the Cooper name returned. But it wasn't until the BMW takeover and the creation of the new MINI that real enthusiasm was involved.

The strategy has worked nicely for BMW, with all those 1960s celebrities who made the original Mini now reflected in the likes of Madonna who own MINIs. Lenses focusing through dark-tinted windows have made out Britney Spears, Peaches Geldof, Danny DeVito, Goldie Hawn and Elijah Wood. Magazines such as *Hello!* and *OK* repeatedly show others and their cars, often in the sort of mild pickle which readers relish. The footballer Didier Drogba returned to his MINI outside Harrods to find a parking ticket on the windscreen. Lord Archer did the same in Cambridge. Vanessa Feltz was nabbed on yellow lines in

Hampstead. Charlotte Church reversed her new MINI into a garden gate during a driving lesson with her grandfather. Lily Allen left a deli with a banana, and drove off munching it, and possibly without due care and attention. More seriously, George Best tested twice over the drink-drive limit in his personalised MINI, G18EST. Away from controversy, MINIs have become the cars which appear in stylish architects' drawings or, less than matchbox size, on their models. They promote Lottery jackpot rollovers. Gordon Brown's small son John drives a MINI pedal car, given to the Prime Minister on a tour of Cowley. It is, of course, a MINI Cooper.

BMW misses nothing in its attempt to invest the fat new baby with the lean, tough aura of the original. In 2004, Cowley produced a limited edition run of 1000 Cooper S cars to commemorate the fortieth anniversary of the first Monte Carlo triumph; they were called MC40s and copied the red and white livery of Hopkirk and company's famous cars. Marketing material was full of words such as 'nimble' and 'pint-sized' and suggested: 'Every driver given the opportunity to take the wheel of a MC40 will feel immediately why entering the Monte Carlo Rally would indeed be a wonderful experience ... Forty years on, nothing has changed.' The cunning branding which marks the 'Build your own Mini' scheme was adapted to include a badge on the bonnet and boot with Hopkirk's 33 EJB registration plate and Monte Carlo symbol. Door roundels with the rally winners' number, 37, were included, magnetic so that they could be removed to foil thieves and souvenir hunters. The gearstick knob carried the fortieth-anniversary badge as well and each car had its own edition number, for all the world like a limited edition of artist's prints. The cars cost £16,600 and they swiftly sold out.

BMW cleverly updated the classic Mini's witty advertising 'stories' – the mediaeval knights on carback and RAF aces chasing 'Hun' Anglias (which BMW might not have countenanced too literally as a remake) – for a series of TV adverts called 'A MINI Adventure'. Keenly marketed, as ever, they won another Guinness record for these, as the shortest feature films (eight seconds) ever made. In 2008 they even boldly commissioned Alan Aldridge to paint a new MINI as he had the old, with his trademark psychedelic patterns and the car divided ying and yanglike into male and female halves. Another special edition had a version of Paul Smith's barcode stripes, but only, cutely, on the back of the wing mirrors.

There was one difference, again typical of BMW's financial nous compared to British vagueness in the Sixties. This time there was no question of Aldridge having to scrub off his masterly work after two days. The painted MINI was part of the Design Museum's four-month Aldridge retro-spective *The Man with Kaleidoscope Eyes* and then took part in the Mini's fiftieth-birthday celebrations. Other canny stunts included a special acknowledgement of the heroic role of Cooper, whose John Cooper Works brand was finally bought by BMW in 2008, allowing JCW MINI Coopers to roll straight off the assembly line. A limited edition, this time of only 200 cars, honoured the fiftieth anniversary of

Jack Brabham's first Formula One victory for John Cooper, with a white and green livery designed by Mike Cooper and based on the racing colours of his father's cars.

If that is cool, the MINI is also ahead of most rivals in a different sort of green; it may be a paradox that cars should figure at all in debates about sustainability, but as we are unable to do without them, it is preferable that they should pollute as little as possible and use the world's supplies of fuel sensibly. Enter the MINI E, with the E standing for Electric, a car which can reach 90mph and has all the other nippy and stylish features of the standard car, but doesn't need petrol or diesel. 'We made them here,' Christian Schoerwerth told me, pointing to a corner of Body and Whites, 'but they went off overseas straight away, for trials. You should have seen their batteries. Enormous! They take up pretty much all the space used by the back seat.'

The E-trials have started in two major centres of 'cool' MINI ownership, New York and Los Angeles, where, for all the grid of yellow-cabbed streets and eight-lane freeways, pioneering part-electric hybrids such as Toyota's Prius have sold very well. Another trial soon followed in Berlin, another popular hub for the car, and now Britain is to follow suit, with a trial in 2010 sponsored by the Government through its arms-length agency, the Technology Strategy Board. Drivers will test 340 electric cars from major companies including Mercedes Benz, which is providing 100 Smart cars in Birmingham, and Peugeot, which will lease forty of its eExpert Teepee people-carriers in Glasgow, helped by forty charging points which Scottish Power is setting up on a temporary basis round the city during the trial. There will also be twenty-one electric sports cars from a consortium of small independent manufacturers – maybe the John Coopers of the future – including a one-off from the wind turbine company Ecotricity which promises, über-greenly, to use only power generated by windfarms. Most demand from would-be volunteers, however, has been for Cowley's forty MINI Es, which will be based in Oxford and nearby counties and monitored by scientists at Oxford Brookes University. Keen to capitalise, as ever, BMW are offering cables to connect trialists' lithium batteries to ordinary three-pin sockets while the car sleeps in the garage and its owners in bed. They also hope to have a 32-amp transformer for domestic use which will cut charging time (for every 150 miles' driving) from ten to four hours.

Fat compared with the old Mini? Yes. Technically, less of a revolution than Issigonis' stroke of genius? Certainly. But the MINI is not only making money, as any product in the private sector should, but also gaining a real hold on drivers' affections. In June this year, the first ever to call at my house in Leeds pulled up. Out of it, just like the adverts for the original Mini's launch, spilled three generations of family friends: a granny, her daughter, two dogs and a bevy of children who gambolled about in the sun. 'Mmmm, yep, they're sweet,' agreed their Mum perfunctorily after we had made the usual complimentary remarks, 'but, look, have you seen our *car*? I've never, ever been interested in cars but I'm getting to love this one very much.' It was only a standard MINI 1 in black, but the spell of the old Mini was there. 'I'm even going online and joining MINI chatrooms,' continued our friend, warming to the subject. 'It's just amazing … it's just … just …'

She tailed off; and final proof of the MINI succession had to wait a couple of weeks and 4,900 miles. It was a sunny morning and Penny and I were trying to cook a tortilla at the El Rey Inn's DIY breakfast bar in Santa Fe, New Mexico. As we stirred and heated, a cheerful-looking woman came in from the sunshine and asked that question so familiar to Brits visiting the United States: 'My! Do you always speak like that? I could just listen to you folks for ever.' She was Marilyn Berg Cooper, a newly retired copy editor from the *Contra Costa Times* at Walnut Creek in San Francisco's Bay Area, who had decided to follow Jack Kerouac and hit the road.

Her wheels? 'Come outside,' she said, and there was a shining dark-blue MINI Cooper, set to loop thousands of miles across the desert to the steamy Gulf states, then hook back up the Eastern seaboard and turn for the West again, across the northern states and down from Seattle to Big Sur. 'I hope I'll make it. I've just checked online and there's not one MINI dealer between Minneapolis and Seattle,' she said calmly. 'I went for twin exhausts, so it doesn't have room for a spare tyre.' But she was an American and full of unquenchable optimism. 'They're supposed to deflate slowly, so I should be OK.' She showed us her registration plate 'Coopers', which she bought years ago in a garage sale on account of her surname, thinking: 'One day I'll find a car for that.'

The day came in 2008 when she read about the new MINI and checked out the system for ordering one online. 'It was just amazing!' she remembered, as she switched on the car's blue-coloured internal lighting. 'There were all these options – colour, fittings, gizmos, God knows what; you could just about design your own car on screen. Then you could log in and check how it was going. They emailed me when work started on *my* car at the factory. And do you guys know, I could check its progress all the way here. I switched on my computer and watched it going through the Panama Canal. It was … it was like having a baby.'

That was the moment which finally won me over to the new MINI; how could anyone stay churlish in the face of Marilyn's radiant pleasure? She had to be off – Amarillo next stop – and we waved her goodbye as the blue jays screeched in the El Rey's garden. 'Will you be OK?' 'Sure I will.' And she and her car were soon a distant dot, catching the sun on the sage.

# Select Bibliography

**Books**

Bardsley, Gillian, *Issigonis: the Official Biography*, Icon Books, 2005

Bobbit, Michael, *Bubblecars and Microcars*, Crowood Press, 2003

Breward, Christopher, Gilbert, David and Lister, Jenny, *Swinging Sixties*, V&A Publications, 2006

Chambers, Maurice; Turner, Stuart; Browning, Peter, *BMC Competitions Department Secrets*, Veloce Publishing, 2005

Levy, Shawn, *Ready, Steady, Go! Swinging London and the invention of cool*, Fourth Estate, 2002

Moss, Pat, *The Story So Far*, William Kimber, 1967

Pomeroy, Laurence, *The Mini Story*, Temple Books 1964

Wood, Jonathan, *Alec Issigonis: the Man who Made the Mini*, Breedon Books, 2005

Wotherspoon, Nick, *'Lawrie' Bond – the man and the marque: the illustrated history of Bond cars*, Bookmarque 1993


**Websites and DVDs**

*www.aronline.co.uk* The matchless online meeting place for enthusiasts for Austin, Rover and related British cars. Packed with knowledgeable articles by owners and veterans of Longbridge, Cowley and elsewhere.

*www.miniownersclub.co.uk* and *www.britishminiclub.co.uk* are among many good and enthusiastic club sites.

*www.malaysiaminilover.com* is a joy among sites run by overseas enthusiasts.

*Mini Fifty*. A compilation of Mini-related films dating back to the 1970s, including BL advertisements. Heritage Motoring Films: *www.motorfilms.com*

*Best of Original Mini*. Includes the separate Austin and Moris promotional films made for the launch in 1959. Heritage Motoring Films: *www.motorfilms.com*

# Index

Aaltonen, Raunoa 18, 132
Adams, Doug 64–6
ADO15 (name of Mini project) 39, 56
Agnelli, Gianni 141, 142, 143
Aldridge, Alan 113–14, 234
*Alec Issigonis: The Man who Made the Mini* (Wood) vii
*Alfie* (film) 141
Amis, Martin 157
Anchors, Tony 'Waspy' 174
Anglia 105E 77
Arctic Mini Run 215
Arica (Chile) 204–5
Arzens, Paul 26
Atkinson, Mr (bubble car owner) 22–3, 24
Atkinson, Rowan 3, 149–50
Austin A35 31, 56
Austin A40 50
Austin Mini-Metro 189–90
Austin Newmarket 56
Austin Se7en 90–1, 105, 110, 123
Austin, Herbert 63, 68–9, 97
Austin Village 63–4
Australia 189, 208–9
Authi (Spanish car builder) 206–7
*Autocar* (magazine) 53, 79, 120, 202

Bailey, David 106
Ballard, J. G. 158–61
Balls, Ed 16
Bambi (bubble car) 26
Bamby (bubble car) 26–7

Banksy (graffiti artist) 161
Bardsley, Gillian vii, 133
Barrass, Jean 15
Batchelor, Jon 197
Bean, David 2, 11
Bean, Graham 1–3, 6–7, 11–12, 16, 20
Bean, Michele 2, 20, 21
Bean, Nicola 2, 11, 12, 20
Beatles, The 112
Beckett, Sir Terence 60, 77–8
Belgium 209
Benn, Anthony Wedgewood 110
Berkeley (bubble car) 27
Best, George 176
Betjeman, John 158
Blanc, Jacques 116
BMW
    and MC40 233
    and the MINI 219–20, 221–4
Bolan, Marc 161–2
Bolan, Rolan 162
Bond, Lawrie 28–9, 36
Bond, Pauline 29
Borden, Iain 108
*Borrowers, The* (film) 152
*Bourne Identity, The* (film) 148–9
Boxer, Marc 113
Brabham, Jack 126, 128–9
British Leyland
    and *The Italian Job* 143
    merger with British Motor Corporation 137
    plans for new Minis 186–7

British Mini Fair 79–88
British Motor Corporation
  and bubble cars 35
  inertia within 31–2
  merger with British Leyland 137
  racing team 131
  staff at 63
  and the Suez Crisis 30–1
British Racing and Sports Car Club
  131
Brooks, Clare 154
Brown, Gordon 16
Brown-Horsley, Holly 168–70
Brown-Horsley, Michael 169
bubble cars
  Bambi 26
  Bamby 26–7
  Berkeley 27
  Bond 27–8
  British 26–7
  and British Motor Corporation 35
  French 26
  Frisky 26
  Goliath 26
  inspired by aircraft design 23–4
  Isetta 35
  Italian 26
  and Lawrie Bond 28–9
  L'Oeuf 26
  Mathis 26
  Messerschmidt Kabinenroller 24,
    25
  and Mike and Paula Cooper 25–7
  Minicar 27–8, 29–30, 35
  Mr Atkinson's 22–3, 24
  Petite 26
  size of 25
  National Bubble Car Museum
    24–5, 27–8, 35
  reverse gear of 25
Bug (customised Mini) 193
Burglar Bill (worker at Longbridge)
  75
Burnley, Audrey 30

Caine, Michael 141, 142, 144
Car (magazine) 209
Carroll family (Mini enthusiasts)
  83–4
Cartledge, Tony 14
Chalgrove airfield (test centre for the
  Mini) 57
Clarkson, Jeremy 20
Charles, Prince 70
Chile 204–6
China, Edd 155
Cobbett, William 44–5
Coleman, Charlotte 147
Collins, Eddie 118
Cooper, Charlie 122, 125, 126
Cooper Climax (racing cars)
  126–7
Cooper, John 10, 109
  and the Cooper Car Company
    126–7
  and Donald Stokes 137–8
  and the MINI 223
  and Mini as a racing car 127–8,
    130, 134, 135
  personality of 124–6
  and the Twini 122
Cooper, Marilyn Berg 237–8
Cooper, Mike and Paula (bubble car
  enthusiasts) 25–7
Coward, Noel 10, 103, 142, 144
Cowley
  bubble car prototype at 35
  industrial relations at 71–3, 98
  making the MINI at 219, 223–30
  Morris Mini-Minors made at 90
  production of Mini stopped 189
  and secret development of the
    Mini 56–7
  working practices in 97–8
Crashed Cars (exhibition) 158–60
Cresswell, Jon 13
Cull, Bill 42, 43–50
Cummings, Ian 228
Curtis, Richard 147

*Daily Mail* (newspaper) 176
*Daily Sketch* (newspaper) 88
Damon, Matt 148, 149
Daniels, Jack 36, 41, 54
Davenport, David 155
Dharmaratnam, Abi 17, 19
Dharmaratnam, Radha 17–19
Dharmaratnam, Suri 17, 19
Diana, Princess 160
Diprose, Ray 66, 71, 72, 73, 74–5
Dodsworth, Trevor 66–7, 71–2, 73, 74
Don, Kaye 125
Doodlebug (racing car) 28–9, 36–7
Doughty, Walter 23
Dowson, Christopher 58
Dowson, George 58
Drago, Jeff 173
Druce, Mr (teacher with interest in
    the Mini) 3–5, 58
Duncan, Frank 45
Duncan, Ian 57

Edmonds, Noel 70, 190
Elizabeth II, Queen 100–1
Enever, Syd 47–8
Erlich, Joseph 51
Evans & Evans (car showroom) 5
Evans, John 194
Evans, Juliet 118, 119
Ewington, Christine 177
Ewington, Danny 176–7, 178

Fabmoc Mini Owners' Club 197
Facorca (Venezuelan company) 203
Faithfull, Marianne 112
Fedden 1Ex (prototype car) 57
Fiat
    Fiat Cinquecento 199
    and *The Italian Job* 141, 142, 143
Flying Flea (miniature plane) 47
Ford Popular 77
*Four Weddings and a Funeral* (film) 147–8
Francis, Geoffrey 113
Frisky (bubble car) 26
Fry, Jeremy 102–3, 104

Garsington (test centre for the Mini)
    57–8
Gay Car of the Year 163
Germany 213
Glenday, Craig 152–3
Goble, Sid 35, 181–2
Godwin, John 146
Goliath (bubble car) 26
Gosling (amphibious jeep) 47
Grant, Hugh 147, 148
Gray, Mike 163
Greenall, Chloe 123
Grice, Bob 50, 51, 52–3, 60–2
Grice, Geoffrey 50, 51
Grice, Robert 50–1
Grint, Rupert 151–2
GT Mini 85–6
Guildford vi

Hall, Alan 27
Hammill, Alison Orchard 162–3
Hardy Spicer (manufacturer of
    universal joints) 48, 49
Harold Radford (coachbuilding
    company) 114–17
Harris family (Mini enthusiasts)
    80–1
Harriman, George 35, 41, 59, 97,
    115, 128, 130
Harrison, George 112
Harvey, Lawrence 113
Hawkins, John 221
Hawthorn, Mike 126
Hayes, Philip 82
Haynes, Roy 185
Hillman Imps 177
Hindley, Myra 160
Hirst, Damien 164–5
Hodge, John 173
Hooper's (livery specialists) 112,
    115–16, 117–18
Hopkirk, Paddy 18, 132–3, 136
Horsman, Frank 98
Huntingdon Area Mini Owners Club
    170

Iles, Martin 179
Iles, Mary 179
*Incredible Seven, The* (promotional film) 91
Inni Minis 201–2
Innocenti Mini-Minor 200–1
International Mini Meet 213, 214–15
Isetta 35
Issigonis, Sir Alec
  biographies of vii
  interest in car design 8–9
  sense of Britishness 9
  lifestyle of 10
  on comfort level of the Mini 12, 98
  on door pockets in the Mini 19–20
  and the Morris Minor 32, 33–4
  and the design of the Mini 34–42
  makes mini-armoured cars 46–7
  and gearbox of the Mini 53
  relationships with co-workers 54–5, 64–5
  and secret development of the Mini 57–9
  and Peter Ustinov 58, 184, 196–7
  working methods of 64–5
  and defects in the Mini 76
  and simplicity of the Mini 94–5
  friendship with Jeremy Fry 102–3
  and Lord Snowdon 103, 104
  and Stirling Moss's test drive 123–4
  and John Cooper 128
  enthusiasm for the Mini as a racing car 132–3
  on the shape of the Mini 174
Issigonis, Constantine (father) 9–10, 36
Issigonis, Demosthenes (grandfather) 9
'Issigonis cell, The' 4, 50, 51–2, 55, 58, 61–3
*Issigonis: The Official Biography* vii
*Italian Job, The* (film) vii, 16, 20, 41, 140–7, 248

Italy 199–202, 208

Japan 212–13
Job, Reg 37
Jones, Gloria 161, 162
Judge, Jan 84–5
Judge, Richard 84–5
Julienne, Remy 145

Keeler, Christine 105
Kennedy Martin, Ian 140, 141
Kennedy Martin, Troy 140–1, 143
Kie, Soong Vic 156
Kimber, Steve vii
Kingsley, Christopher 129–30
Knowledale Car Club Mini Miglia 131

Lampredi, Aurelio 95, 123
Leeds Classic Mini Owners' Club vii, 11, 158
Leigh, Richard 82
Lennon, John 112, 113, 115
Lickey Hills (test ground for Mini) 51, 56
Lightweight Special (sports car) 46, 124, 132
Little Guy (customised Mini) 191
L'Oeuf (bubble car) 26
London-Brighton 'Palace to Pier' run 11, 12
'London Spot Mini' (Hirst) 164–5
Longbridge
  decline of 60, 222
  industrial relations at 71–3
  'Issigonis cell' at 4, 50, 51–2, 61–3
  and the MINI 224–5
  and secret development of the Mini 4–5, 37, 55–9
  size of 68
  workforce camaraderie at 74–5
  working practices in 97–8
Lord, Sir Leonard 22, 31–3, 34, 36, 37, 40, 59, 76, 93, 128

Lucas (engineering firm) 54–5
Lynn, Dame Vera vi

Maan, Jasween Kaur 156
Macmillan, Harold 31
Makinen, Timo 18, 134, 135
Malta 213, 214
Manders, Colin 67–8, 69–70, 190
Mandry, Robert 187–8
Margaret, Princess 101, 103–5
Margrave (customised Mini) 117–18
Marples, Ernie 110
Marsh, David 62
Marshall, Frank 148
Mathis (bubble car) 26
MC40 233
McCartney, Paul 112, 115
McQueen, Steve 111–12, 211
Meadows, Shane 150
*Meditation on the A30* (Betjeman) 158
MegaMini (customised Mini) 193–4
Messerschmidt Kabinenroller (bubble car) 24, 25
Michelmore, Cliff 132
Millennium Vault, Guildford vi
Mills, Bruce 86
Mini
    advertising for 178–9
    in the Antarctic 215
    in the Arctic 215–16
    in Australia 189, 208–9
    in Belgium 209
    and Bill Cull 48–50
    boot space in 21
    in *The Bourne Identity* 148–9
    built overseas 199–209
    carburettor in 75
    celebrity backing for 100–9, 111–14
    chrome strip on 65
    clubs for 197, 206
    comfort levels of 12
    and congestion in London 109–11
    cramming into 152–7
    cross-generational appeal of 13, 20

customising 112–18, 164, 191–4
design of 7–9, 34–42
difficulties on the assembly line 66–8, 69–70, 71, 75–7
Donald Stokes' hostility to 137–8
door pockets in 19–20
engine choice 51–2
exhibitions involving 158–61, 164–6
export market for 96–7, 136
in *Four Weddings and a Funeral* 147–8
as 'gay' car 163–4
gears of 52–3
in Germany 213
high speed modifications to 127–30
as icon of the 1960s 105, 108–9
interior size of 1–3, 5, 12, 19
in *The Italian Job* 140–7
in Italy 199–202, 208
in Japan 212–13
and John Cooper 127–8, 130–1
launch of 90–2, 98–9
literary owners of 157
in Malta 213, 214
and Mary Quant 106–8, 164
in Mr Bean television series 149–50
poetry about 157–8
police use of 174–8
press reactions to 88–90
price of 77
production costs of 76–8
prototype names of 39, 56, 59
as racing car 127–35, 138–9
and railways 111
royal backing for 100–2, 103–5, 106
safety of 16–19
sales of 78, 135–7, 190
secret development of 4–5, 37, 55–9
simplicity of 93–5
in South America 202–6

in Spain 206–8
speed of 16, 20
speedometer in 65
stretch Minis 171–4
suspension of 53–4
in television programmes 151
in *Thunderpants* 151–2
transverse engine 4, 30–42, 75
in the United States 93, 210–12
and universal joints of 41–2,
    48–50
water leaking problems 75–6, 88
wheels of 53
world record attempts using
    152–7, 194–5
MINI, The 7, 138, 163–4
    advertising for 233–4
    and Alan Aldridge 233–4
    assembly line for 223–30
    and BMW 221–4
    celebrity backing for 232
    comparison with the old Mini
        217–18
    customising 229–31, 237
    disliked by Mini owners 218–19
    MINI Cooper 234, 237
    MINI E 234–6
Mini 1275GT 185–6
Mini A+ 1
Mini Bel Air (customised Mini) 115,
    116
Mini City 82
Mini Clubman 138, 181
MINI Cooper 234, 237
Mini Cooper 14, 17, 123, 130–2,
    134–7, 144, 148, 149, 153,
    156, 167, 176–7, 211, 231–2
Mini Cooper S 111, 112, 133, 138,
    145, 153, 178
Mini Cord 202–3
Mini Countryman 180–1, 191
Mini De Luxe (customised Mini)
    115, 116
Mini de Villes (customised Mini) 115
MINI E 235–6

*Mini Freak* (Japanese fan magazine)
    212–13
Mini Grande Luxe (customised Mini)
    115
Mini Mark I 87
Mini Mark II 111, 116, 184–5
Mini Mark III 189
Mini Mark IV 189
Mini Mayfair 15, 16, 83
Mini-Moke 181–3, 208–9
Mini Pickup 180
Mini Shorty 168–71
Mini Sprite 82
*Mini Story, The* (Pomeroy) vii, 103,
    104, 174
Mini-trac 215
Mini Traveller 180–1, 191
Minicar (bubble car) 27–8, 29–30,
    35
Minitour (customised Mini) 193
Minivan 87, 150, 174–5, 179–80
Minshull, Len 118
Mr Bean television series 149–50
Molly Mini (children's books) 162–3
Mongol Rally 197–8
Monte Carlo rallies 18, 29, 132,
    134–5
Morris, John 58
Morris, Marcus 108–9
Morris Mini-Minor 90–1, 110, 152
Morris Minor 31, 32, 33–4, 37–8,
    40–1, 57, 63, 211
Morris, William *see* Nuffield, Lord
Moss, Kate 164
Moss, Pat 131
Moss, Stirling 29, 123–4, 126, 131
*Motor, The* (magazine) 89, 95–6, 113,
    115, 122
Motor Heritage Museum 51, 93,
    123, 135, 186
*Motor Trend* (magazine) 211
Moulton, Alex 53, 54, 61
Moulton, John Coney 53–4
Mudlark (amphibious jeep) 47
Musgrave, H. J. 70

Nanjing Motor Corporation 60, 68
National Bubble Car Museum 24–5, 27–8, 35
National Mini/MINI Owners Club viii
Nesmith, Mike 116
Nicholl-Griffiths, Hubert Victor 88
Nuffield, Lord 33, 97

Oak, Vic 37
O'Hare, Terry 215
*Once Upon A Time in the Midlands* (TV series) 150
Orange Box (prototype name for the Mini) 59
Osborne, Ken 38
Ottley, Ian 81–2
*Oxford English Dictionary* 118–21

Paradise, Filmer 137
Paris Motor Show 56
Paul, Henri 160
Pellandine, Peter 187–9
Perry, Christine 3, 4, 5, 10–11, 87, 89, 179
Petite (bubble car) 26
Pickett, Les 117, 118
Pininfarina, Battista 95
Pischetsrieder, Bernd 222–3, 224
Place, Andy 197, 198
Plunket, Alexander 107
Pomeroy, Lawrence vii, 31, 40, 53, 95–6, 99
Poole, Jack 49
Pressed Steel Fisher site (Oxford) 219–21
*Prisoner, The* (television series) 183
Profumo, John 105

Quant, Mary 106–8, 121, 164

Radford, Harold 115–16, 118
Read, Dan vii
Read, Luan vii, 154–5, 156–7
Reading Ladies rugby team 153–6

Rice-Davies, Mandy 105
Richmond, Daniel 127–8
Riddle, Donald 36
Riley Elf 48, 90, 137, 173, 183–4
Riley Pathfinder 50
Robertson, Steve 120
Robinson, Derek ('Red Robbo') 72–3
Robinson, Geoffrey 200–1, 208
Rolling Stones 112
Rolls Royce Jimmy (worker at Longbridge) 75
*Room for Romeo Brass, A* (film) 150
Russell, Malcolm 38
Rzeppa, Alfred 44
Rzeppa House 43

Saatchi, Charles 164–5
Sailor Bill (worker at Longbridge) 74
Salamander (armoured car) 47
Salt, Titus 45
Saltaire 45
*Saturday Night at the London Palladium* 133–4
Scamp, The (kit car) 187
Schreider, Doreen 63
Schroerwerth, Christian 224, 225, 226, 234–5
Scott, Alfred 45, 46
Sellers, Peter 105, 109, 112–13
Sheppard, John 56
Shipley (nr. Bradford) 43, 44–5
Simpson, John 119–20, 121
*Small Car and Mini Owner* (magazine) 109
Smith, Sidney 35
Snowdon, Lord 101–2, 103–5, 106, 111
Sociable (three-wheeled car) 47
South America 202–6
Spacey, Kevin 172
Spain 206–8
Spice Girls, The 173–4
Spooner, William 45
*Sports Graphic* (magazine) 211

Squirrel (motorbike) 47
Stangroom, Angela 221
Starr, Ringo 112, 115
Stokes, Donald 137–8
*Sunday Times, The* (newspaper) 113

Tarbuck, Jimmy 134–5
Taylor-Haynes, Lindsay 171–2
Thomas, Sir Miles 33, 38
*Thunderpants* (film) 151–2
*Times, The* (newspaper) 109, 190
Tomaso, Alejandro de 201
*Top Gear* (magazine) vii
Tour de France rallies 132–3, 134, 136
Townsend, Peter 101
Trimini (customised Mini) 192
Triumph 1300 118
Troth, David 86–7
Turner, Stuart 131, 133
Twini (experimental Mini) 122, 125

Unipower 47–8
United States of America 93, 210–12
Ustinov, Peter 58, 184, 196–7

Vargas, Victor 202
Venezuela 202–3
VW Beetle 210–11

Wade, Scott 165–6
Wagner, Lindsay 151
Wainwright, Penny 13, 81, 86, 88, 109, 236
Wainwright, Tom 13, 14–16
Wakefield, Sir Peter 209
Waldorf, Stephen 160
Watts, Doug 129
Wheeler, Peter 48, 49
Wight, Robin 7
Wilson, Gordon 211
*Wizardry on Wheels* (promotional film) 91
Wolseley Hornet 137, 183–4
Wolfe, Tom 107
Wood, Bill 117, 118
Wood, Carl 22
Wood, Jonathan vii
'Works, The' *see* Longbridge plant
Wright, Ian 154
Young, Will 161

## Italian Job solution

John Godwin's winning entry in the Royal Society of Chemistry competition solved the teetering coach problem like this: The gang smash the windows at the rear of the coach using something like a shoe; the glass falls outwards, removing its weight from the overhanging part of the coach. They reach out and smash the front windows inwards, adding their weight to the section grounded on top of the cliff. One gang member is lowered to the ground to let the air out of the front tyres, settling the coach on the ground. The pipe to the fuel tank is slashed, draining an estimated 36 gallons of diesel from the overhanging rear. That would remove another 130kg (286lb), allowing a 90kg man to start removing the gold bars. *Quod erat demonstrandum.*

Four runners-up suggested piling up limestone rocks as a counter-balance, making acid from the safe-blowing explosive to dissolve a small amount of gold (a sacrifice justified by the salvage of the rest), igniting leaked fuel to melt the road's surface and glue the coach down, and getting the gang to move right to the front which would allow one to salvage the gold. The proponent of the last solution went to the lengths of discovering that the Bedford coach's front bumper would have been too narrow for gang members to stand on, but argued that they would form a sufficient counterweight if they crammed into the driver's cabin. The Royal Society of Chemistry wasn't convinced. After all, it was Michael Caine's shambolic crew, not the Reading Ladies rugby team.